FONTANE

Praise for the

It was only a matter of time before a clever publisher realized that there is an audience for whom *Exile on Main Street* or *Electric Ladyland* are as significant and worthy of study as *The Catcher in the Rye* or *Middlemarch* . . . The series . . . is freewheeling and eclectic, ranging from minute rock-geek analysis to idiosyncratic personal celebration—*The New York Times Book Review*

Ideal for the rock geek who thinks liner notes just aren't enough—*Rolling Stone*

One of the coolest publishing imprints on the planet—*Bookslut*

These are for the insane collectors out there who appreciate fantastic design, well-executed thinking, and things that make your house look cool. Each volume in this series takes a seminal album and breaks it down in startling minutiae. We love these. We are huge nerds—*Vice*

A brilliant series . . . each one a work of real love—*NME* (UK)

Passionate, obsessive, and smart—*Nylon*

Religious tracts for the rock 'n' roll faithful—*Boldtype*

[A] consistently excellent series—*Uncut* (UK)

We . . . aren't naive enough to think that we're your only source for reading about music (but if we had our way . . . watch out). For those of you who really like to know everything there is to know about an album, you'd do well to check out Bloomsbury's "33 1/3" series of books—*Pitchfork*

For almost 20 years, the 33-and-a-Third series of music books has focused on individual albums by acts well known (Bob Dylan, Nirvana, Abba, Radiohead), cultish (Neutral Milk Hotel, Throbbing Gristle, Wire) and many levels in-between. The range of music and their creators defines "eclectic," while the writing veers from freewheeling to acutely insightful. In essence, the books are for the music fan who (as Rolling Stone noted) "thinks liner notes just aren't enough."—*The Irish Times*

For reviews of individual titles in the series, please visit our blog at 333sound.com and our website at https://www.bloomsbury.com/uk/academic/music-sound-studies/
Follow us on Twitter: @333books
Like us on Facebook: https://www.facebook.com/33.3books

For a complete list of books in this series, see the back of this book.

Forthcoming in the series:

and many more . . .

Fontanelle

Selena Chambers

BLOOMSBURY ACADEMIC
NEW YORK · LONDON · OXFORD · NEW DELHI · SYDNEY

BLOOMSBURY ACADEMIC
Bloomsbury Publishing Inc
1385 Broadway, New York, NY 10018, USA
50 Bedford Square, London, WC1B 3DP, UK
29 Earlsfort Terrace, Dublin 2, Ireland

First published in the United States of America 2023

Library of Congress Cataloging-in-Publication Data

Names: Chambers, Selena, author.
Title: Fontanelle / Selena Chambers.
Description: New York: Bloomsbury Academic, 2023. | Series: 33 1/3 | Includes bibliographical
references. | Summary: "Puts Babes in Toyland in the context of women's music, ranging from Sappho
through Neo-Riot Grrl, with the goal of providing a more universal and inclusive narrative for all rock
history"– Provided by publisher.
Identifiers: LCCN 2022031252 (print) | LCCN 2022031253 (ebook) | ISBN 9781501377556 (paperback) |
ISBN 9781501377563 (epub) | ISBN 9781501377570 (pdf) | ISBN 9781501377587 (ebook other)
Subjects: LCSH: Babes in Toyland (Musical group). Fontanelle. | Punk rock music–United States–History
and criticism. | Grunge music–United States–History and criticism.
Classification: LCC ML421.B23 C43 2023 (print) | LCC ML421.B23 (ebook) |
DDC 782.42166092/2–dc23/eng/20220802
LC record available at https://lccn.loc.gov/2022031252
LC ebook record available at https://lccn.loc.gov/2022031253

ISBN: PB: 978-1-5013-7755-6
ePDF: 978-1-5013-7757-0
eBook: 978-1-5013-7756-3

Series: 33⅓

Typeset by Deanta Global Publishing Services, Chennai, India
Printed and bound in Great Britain

To find out more about our authors and books visit www.bloomsbury.com and sign up
for our newsletters.

For Jena, Juli, Landa, Lisa, Sarah, and Regina

Contents

Intro
Soft Spots

Babes in Toyland's major-label debut, *Fontanelle* (1992), is one of the most impactful and forgotten albums of the 1990s. Presenting a raw and violent female catharsis rarely expressed even in today's fourth-wave feminist works, it has become almost all but forgotten in grunge-music and girl-band retrospectives, as have Babes in Toyland's importance as a whole. Despite creating a unique brand of sisterhood that inspired women to create bands of their own such as L7, Hole, Bikini Kill, and 7 Year Bitch, the Babes' story now seems to only exist as footnotes to other more famous figures and acts.

Bikini Kill's Kathleen Hanna lamented in a 2010 interview: "In the 90s, Babes in Toyland was a band that was hugely important to us and we were like, God, if only we could play awesome shows like Babes in Toyland. And now, you know, I meet girls who have no idea who they are. And I watch them be erased."[1]

In Hanna's quote, today's reader might infer that those who are erasing Babes in Toyland are men, but I believe their erasure has more to do with women. During the time of Babes' rise, there was an ongoing conversation within the media of the significance of all-girl bands as vehicles for furthering the feminist agenda. Some aspects of media led these conversations in positive ways, but other aspects of the discussion also served the mainstream media's efforts at a feminist backlash. The Babes have always maintained that their music had no political agenda other than what was personal. The band and its music weren't meant to be read as any sort of feminist manifesto, and because politics weren't their intent, they refused to participate in the conversations that most concerned them at the time. As a result, feminists aren't exactly talking about Babes in Toyland.

While everyone at the time got sick of being asked "What does it mean to be a girl in a band" and "Are you a feminist?," bands like L7, Hole, and Bikini Kill leaned in to the coverage with feminist-conscious statements about their work. I believe this is where a lot of the Babes' erasure stems from. Their more media-savvy peers provided quotable and thought-provoking copy, while the Babes' adamant focus on their music gave them less intellectual copy to resource for feminist think-pieces and histories like riot grrl slogans, L7's Rock the Choice campaign, and Courtney Love's "football captain" speech.

There was one aspect of media focus the Babes did unfortunately and reluctantly participate in—the infamous battle of the dress with Hole frontwoman Courtney Love. It was a sensational and inane expression of the media's love of pitting strong women against each other, and because it came to its height during *Fontanelle*'s promotion, it became the dominating narrative of this band. There have been numerous opportunities to correct this, but most have failed.

One recent example can be found in *Rolling Stone's* "Top 50 Greatest Grunge Albums," published in 2019. *Fontanelle* was ranked at number 33, but rather than talk about the strengths of the band or the album's importance, they rehashed the tabloid backlash about Love and the dress (and this from one of the roundtable's female critics).[2] And that's really too bad, because while the Babes never felt comfortable saying much about their work, there is plenty to say about it as well as much to learn from it.

While the Babes weren't screaming "women's rights" during their sets or in interviews, they were screaming about the pain and struggle they experienced as women within the patriarchy. And they were doing this within a male-dominated arena without "trying to be like the guys" or even trying to out do them. The fact that the Babes were only in competition with themselves within a highly competitive musical scene and industry was a radical act of feminism. This created an inspiring example to other women that a female space for the female imagination was possible, and with no training necessary! This spurred women to pick up guitars, get behind the drums, and find their own voices and empowerment through music divorced of the male gaze and its censoring and condescending expectations.

They screamed in a way that said more about the oppression women experienced within their individual lives than most feminist manifestos. They crafted a unique and primal noise complimented by a violently vulnerable aesthetic that made for extreme reactions of either admiration or repulsion by people who experienced their sound. Their stage presence was not polite or catering—

rather their music raged with lyrical swears spat like hexes and an emotional range that hovered between operatic scales and serpentine exorcism—always playing as loud and hard as they could. Through all this, Babes in Toyland have as much intellectual capital within feminist discussions as any other women artists of their time. But to find it, you have to do what the Babes have been asking everyone to do all along—look at their art.

I say art and not music because there is a complete package to the band that is often not discussed. There is the sound created by each woman's individual playing style, Bjelland's lyrics that drive the cathartic turns of each song, and there is the collaborative effort toward a feminine aesthetic that cleverly turns the backlash against itself in the same way as the works of Barbara Kruger and Cindy Sherman did at the time. (It is no coincidence that Sherman provided the cover for *Fontanelle* and its EP follow-up *Painkillers*.) All of this, plus the inspiring examples made by their ethos, is all perfectly showcased within *Fontanelle*.

Sutured Experiences

"Fontanelle" refers to the soft spots on a baby's head where the connective membranes, called sutures, haven't fully fused the skull's five plates together. While this facilitates passing through the birth canal passage, and allows the baby's brain to develop during its seminal first year, it also means that there are two vulnerable oculi at the front and back of the skull that requires up to two years to completely heal when the skull plates are fully fused together. This leaves the infant vulnerable to potential brain damage if care isn't taken.[3]

This book is structured around the idea of the Fontanelle, with the five plates presenting the factual aspects of the Babes' story while recording their major-label debut, and the two soft spots as the areas of the album and band's coverage that has been lacking throughout their entire history. The sutures, of course, are the clearing of those areas that have been fabricated, sensationalized, or misunderstood in-between the benchmark biographical moments and artistic achievements.

These two areas of the Babes' career represent what was damaged by the media's feminist backlash, or ignored by current feminist and music histories. The hope with this study, and this metaphor, is to regenerate discussion (the sutures) of their music within a new appreciation of their contribution to an important feminist zeitgeist within music that explored the vulnerabilities of girlhood and its societal fetishization into womanhood. This was explored in the dress and antics of many female performers during this time, like Daisy Chainsaw's KatieJane Garside and other Kinderwhore icons. But through the Babes' take, Kinderwhore went beyond frontwoman Kat Bjelland's vintage dresses and goldilocks features to explore a much darker and violent undercurrent than the twee celebrations its fashions have implied. Among some of the Babes' darker meditations are their ironic use of childhood nostalgia—gendered games and toys—juxtaposed by aggressive songs depicting abuse, addiction, abandonment, and animosity solely from female experience and perspective.

In the Anterior Fontanelle chapter, the sutures fuse the development of this aesthetic expression and the influence it had on their female peers. The Posterior Fontanelle chapter zooms in further on this discussion by divorcing Bjelland from the backlash narratives that plagued her and refocusing on her own personal spin on femininity through her complexity and genius as a lyricist.

Mixed Metaphors

Babes in Toyland's biography is something else in need of making whole, but remains fragmented and incomplete. Their story has never accurately been told thanks to fading memory, media indifference, and disproportionate perspectives presented by the band members. Drummer Lori Barbero has always been vocal about her experience within interviews. The bassists, both writers, have been willing to weigh in with their autobiographies—Michelle Leon has presented her version in *I Live Inside: Memoir of A Babe in Toyland*, and Maureen Herman is finishing up her book, *It's a Memoir, Motherfucker*, as of this writing. But while each member has tried to tell their side of it, each take further obscures the whole, making the history feel fragmented at times, especially since frontwoman Kat Bjelland is notoriously reclusive, and Tim Carr, the bands A&R person for Reprise/Warner Brothers, tragically died in 2017. There are aspects of this story that, thirty years after recording *Fontanelle*, would have certainly been made clearer by their perspectives.

The only book dealing solely with Babes in Toyland as a band up until now is Neal Karlen's 1994 authorized biography *Babes in Toyland: The Making and Selling of a Rock and Roll Band*. It follows the Babes from 1991 to 1993, and provides pertinent, behind-the-scenes information on the inner workings of recording a major record label, like *Fontanelle*. But, it bares stating that all of the members of the Babes, and others portrayed in the book, have all disputed its depiction of certain exchanges and dramatization of events. Even so, Karlen continues to stand by his account of this time[4] and as his biography deals specifically with *Fontanelle*, I do reference him in this study alongside where it is collaborated by the newer accounts, interviews, and texts from the past thirty years, as well as my own conversations with Lori Barbero, Maureen Herman, Michelle Leon, Lee Ranaldo, and Brian Paulson that were conducted from 2021 to 2022.

While I have tried to piece things together more cohesively where I could and strike a balance through the years, straight biography is not the intent of this book. My hope is to create a better appreciation of the band's importance during their heyday and what their significance is to *our* day. For at the band's core was a fierce and unique feminine ethos that they presented and promoted through their performances and work. Not only do they show the possibilities and potentials of an all-female space and imagination, but beyond gender, they offer everyone a reminder that internal resistance is every bit as important as external resistance.

Art doesn't have to be political to be radical, and more often than not most revolutions begin within one's internal struggle that unintentionally creates relatable experiences within others that then become translated into political change, or at least progressive conversation and cultural exchange. This is what makes a band like Babes in Toyland, who draw so poignantly from their life experiences of abuse and betrayal, feel so radical that it is hard to believe they had no political intent. Or why simply their presentation as three independent and subversive women occupying what was predominantly the male stage could feel natural to them but stir revolutionary fire within their female audience.

The Babes followed their bliss in a way that many women hadn't imagined at the time—and this was a revelation. They didn't let patriarchal notions of perfectionism, competition, and "a woman's place" prevent them from picking up their instruments and taking lessons from their soul while on stage and on the road. They challenged themselves and supported each other to grow—and in doing so each woman became unique and revered stylists of their time. They weren't afraid to seem ugly or off-putting, instead they elevated the unfeminine emotions of rage, angst, and wrath into sublime expression. Perhaps most radically—they were doing this because it was fun, self-fulfilling, and really because *they believed they could*. They were babes in the universe—curious, fearless, and ready to explore.[5]

These key components of the spirit behind their music are all things that have become easy to lose sight of in today's dog-eat-dog, gig economy where all passions are commodified online. While the Babes did end up making some money from their music—turning the fun into work—they still remained uncompromised to their core ethos. And while they avoided leaning into the feminist keyword, feminism needs Babes in the discussion. Not just because they are an exemplary model for the power and potential of how the feminine imagination can thrive within a female space, but of the might and resilience of three human beings who happened to be female and refused to let that build up walls around their dreams and ambitions.

Plate 1
The Coolest Girls in the World

The band was conceived in 1986 at a backyard barbecue in Minneapolis. Lori Barbero had seen Kat Bjelland around since Bjelland's arrival that summer: "She was always at the afterparties, at the shows, and was usually one of the only girls that was there like me."[1] While Bjelland was new to town, Barbero was a Minneapolis native. She spent her high school years in New York City, where she explored the rich glam and punk scenes thriving at that time, seeing live performances by David Bowie, Queen, and Patti Smith.

She returned to Minneapolis in 1980 to enroll at the University of Minnesota. She began taking an active role within the Heyday—the innovative and groundbreaking local punk scene burgeoning around her—and she dropped out of school to wait tables at the Longhorn Bar, the nexus of this musical explosion. At Longhorn, she could be paid while supporting her friends on stage or watching the legendary acts passing through. Eventually, Longhorn extended its stage to what would become First Avenue, and Barbero extended her couch at her home, known as "Big Trouble House," to almost every band that played there.

So when Kat Bjelland started showing up at First Avenue and hanging around backstage, Barbero noticed the newcomer instantly. Barbero at first found her stand-offish: "She was at a lot of shows, but always off to the side and off by herself. . . . She'd never talk to me, she never looked at me, but she was just uncomfortable and shy and introverted, but she always talked to the boys."[2]

She wouldn't know it until later, but Bjelland had been looking at Barbero.

"I came to Minneapolis from San Francisco," Bjelland recalled in 1992,

and I didn't really know anybody . . . . And I saw Lori dancing at First Avenue all the time, just by herself, a really great dancer, she had really good rhythm. And then I met her at a barbecue party and I said: "Do you know how to play drums?" And she said: "I have a set, but she didn't know how to play." I thought perfect. She's going to be perfect.[3]

"What the fuck is this?"

Bjelland had come to Minneapolis solely to make music. While Barbero had never been in a band before, Bjelland had been in half a dozen: "I just wanted to go somewhere. I used to work at this club in Portland, and bands that used to come there from Minneapolis were really cool."[4]

Bjelland had come from a broken and abusive family in Salem, Oregon, and found solace in music. She was disappointed when gifted an acoustic guitar in second grade because she wanted an electric one.[5] Her wish would go unfulfilled until high school: "My first boyfriend was a metal-head guy, kind of—he played a Flying-V, and he had a Marshall and a Hi-Watt he left in my basement. Whenever he'd leave, I'd just pick it up. . . . You know how powerful those things are? I was like, '*Fuck! This is for me! I've gotta do this!*'"[6] For instruction, she turned to her musician-uncle David Higginbotham who taught her the "basics of melody . . . campfire songs . . ." as well as surf riffs and songwriting. Beyond his lessons, she'd pick out the tunes from favored bands like The B-52s, The Cramps, and The Divinyls.

She learned on his Gibson ES-335, and struggled with the large neck. This led her to seek out a more suitable instrument, and she found the perfect fit in a pawned red Rickenbacker 425 (some say 420). Once an icon of 1960s rock via The Beatles and other mods—it would become reborn as a grunge avatar throughout her career: "I think she selected the Rick[enbacker]," Higginbotham explained on a YouTube AMA, "because of it's [sic] small size (Kat is not a large person) and probably because of it's [sic] angular shaping - smoothed and rounded shapes and forms were not embraced by the punk movement."[7]

The Neurotics was Kat's first official band, and it was a surf band that included her best friend at the time Laura Robertson on bass, Uncle David as lead guitarist, Bjelland on rhythm, Brian McMillan on drums, and Marty Wyman on vocals.[8]

The band seems to have had several performances. Their first gig at Flight 99 was Bjelland's inauguration on the stage, and while Higginbotham claims there are audio recordings, none have surfaced as of this writing. However, the surf rock influence, as well as the rockabilly licks picked up from the Cramps and the B-52s, alongside Bjelland's evolution into punk, can be heard in her next band, The Venarays.

It is important to note that somewhere in-between The Neurotics and The Venarays, Bjelland found punk rock. Portland was a West Coast equivalent of the Minneapolis Heyday, and Bjelland would drive down to catch the acts. Her first exposure to punk was local band, The Wipers, one of the Pacific Northwest's first punk bands and pioneers of the "Seattle" sound.

Up until now, Bjelland had only really been exposed to mainstream, hard rock like Rush, Kiss, Led Zeppelin, and Aerosmith.[9] The Wipers was a descent into the underground. They were heavy but tuneful—distorted hooks, gritty riffs, and hauntingly melodic lyrics—a bridge between punk and new wave. It was something Bjelland had never encountered before: "I felt like the world opened up . . . I didn't know about punk rock that much. I was from a small town. All of a sudden I was like, 'What the f[uck] is this?'"[10]

She took this noisy epiphany and applied it to The Venarays: "I got this band together with my best friends, so it was an all-girl band . . . . We began as a way of having fun with each other."[11] There's a single performance available online from a Woodburn Public Access show. It features a band interview and a six-song set: "Catatonic," "Timebomb," "I Hate You," "Bite Your Tongue," "Put To The Test," and "Go Back To Him."

In the performance, Bjelland is already experimenting with what will eventually become her iconic look, but at the moment it's more like a Goth Patrick Nagal print than a Carole Baker movie poster—dark pixie hair, kohl-lined eyes, and slasher red lips that matched the red Rickenbacker strap sashing her black vintage sweater dress. She's reserved in the interview, but informs the host: "We play about 90% originals [written by her], and its pretty raw because there's only one guitar and one bass so I don't play many leads. So it's kind of a little bit 60s, it just has that edge to it, a 60s edge."[12] The trio ensemble is one of the major distinctions Bjelland learned from surf to punk—most punk bands at the time were trios, making the sound more rhythmic and cacophonic than the melodic wave-washing of multi-guitar surf rock melodies.

The band is pretty decent. Frontwoman Marty Wyman's voice has the same kind of melodic strain that could have easily bridged The Runaways to Siouxsie and the Banshees. There are some abrasive, purposely tone-deaf songs that are the imitations of The Wipers and other punk bands, but you can tell that the Woodburn girls are having a hard time shaking off their surf rock roots.

Those influences are most apparent in "I Hate You" and "Catatonic." Other songs like "Bite Your Tongue" serve up more of a Satyricon vibe with a vitriolic cheerleading squad chant that are Bjelland's only vocals. The band seems pulled in several musical directions, and it's little wonder their momentum—which was landing them gigs at Satyricon opening for groundbreaking bands like Napalm Beach—didn't last.[13]

Bjelland was undeterred. During her time with The Venarays, she had moved to Eugene to attend the University of Oregon, but again like Barbero in Minneapolis, dropped out her freshman year to pursue the scene. She relocated to Portland in 1982 and stripped to support herself: "It was the only job which allowed me to travel and work my own hours while making enough money to do exactly what I wanted to do."[14] It gave her the time she needed to work on her poetry and songwriting, and it would carry her through many hard times during her musical career: "It makes you more aware of how you can wrap people round your finger and it's probably made me more aware of the body, which has probably influenced my lyrics, because the whole time I've been in a band I've been stripping."[15]

Around this time, she grew dissatisfied with The Venarays, and left them to sit on jams in The Ex-Rays, her Uncle's new band post-Neurotics. She wouldn't form another band of her own until summer 1984, when one night at The Satyricon, she looked down on the floor and found Courtney Love looking back up at her: "She fell to my feet, grabbed my ankles and said 'Please be in my band and be my guitarist.'"[16]

From Sugar Babylon to Italian Whorenuns

Newly returned to her hometown, Love was blown away by the new Venaray's girl shredding on stage, and wanted her to be in her band, Sugar Babylon. After some hesitation, Bjelland agreed and they relocated together to San Francisco, recruited bassist Jennifer Finch, added a drummer, and rebranded as Sugar Babydoll.

It went nowhere. After Finch quit and went on to found L7, Love and Bjelland reincarnated the band for a third time as Pagan Babies with Deirdre Schletter (drums) and Janis Tanaka (bass). The new iteration released a dream pop/new wave four-track demo before Love quit in protest. Janis had turned Bjelland onto the raging, all-female San Francisco band, Frightwig—another musical revelation: "This is who got me going, actually, this is who inspired me to start a band." While The Wipers showed Bjelland that there was craftsmanship in sloppiness, Frightwig demonstrated that women could be just as skilled or chaotic and angry as any male band: "they were just kind of making a big racket too, so I thought I could do that."[17]

It was after encountering Frightwig, at the end of 1985, that she began experimenting with what would become known as her definitive style. Love hated this new direction, and quit the band with famous last words: "You're never gonna get anywhere making that punk rock noise."[18] Obviously, Love would later revise this stance and proclaim she was as inspired by Frightwig as Tanaka and Bjelland were.[19]

Undeterred by Love's prediction, Bjelland, Tanaka, and Schletter renamed themselves the Italian Whorenuns. If the previous bands with Love had been incubators for Bjelland, this last incarnation was the accelerator towards what would fuel Babes in Toyland. While The Venarays laid the instrumental foundation for Bjelland's evolving style, what was missing was moving her voice to the front.

In the Italian Whorenuns, Bjelland steps up to the mic and screams for long durations in the songs like "Ice Cream and Cigarettes" and "You Got it." In "I Hate You," originally a Venaray's song sung by Wyman, the full potential of her ranges—from guttural grunts, spitting hisses, and cutie-pie melodies—are beginning to be showcased. When you compare the fast rockabilly licks of "I Hate You" with Babes in Toyland's "Spit to See the Shine," you realize that over time Bjelland maintains her surf rockabilly roots, but slows those tropes down to a drunken crawl, giving Babes in Toyland that swampy viscosity that's so unique to their sound.

Despite this huge artistic shift, Bjelland was not satisfied with the Italian Whorenuns demo and their few performances. In fact, she was weary of the entire scene. In only a few years, she'd been in five bands, and with the exception of The Venarays, those bands' patterns were: play dress up for pictures, maybe record some demos, and have a one-night stand at a venue before breaking up. Bjelland felt like her efforts were going nowhere. She had loved all of the Minneapolis bands that came through Portland; she was willing to bet she'd find the band she was looking for out there.

The First Practice

Despite her passion for music, Barbero had never played an instrument. Shortly before befriending Bjelland, she had just bought a drum-set off friends from Run Westy Run on a lark: "They stayed in a walk in closet for a long time, and they just sat in there all set up."[20]

By all accounts, the practices were fun and sometimes cryptic, like when: "There was a starling in the basement and at the end of the rehearsal it was dead in the corner."[26] Nothing sums up the sonic sound the women were developing better than this.

No Pussyfoot Kind of Band

The women practiced in a basement and premiered in another weeks later.[27] It's a mundane factoid that I love thinking about. While this choice of practice space was more about convenience, I can't help but think about the significance of it as a sacred creative space.

It obviously calls to mind Virginia Woolf's "a room of one's own," but also Kathleen Hannah's musical variation: "I needed to get used to the sound of my own voice [for The Julie Ruin], and I think that's what makes a girl's bedroom special. You can make whatever you want when you're alone in your room."[28]

And it being underground feels so mythical to me—just like many a Goddess before them, they had to go under to reinvent themselves. They could leave their public and social lives above, while below they experimented, fucked up, goofed off, and jammed out until they started finding a sound that felt right. While the world above still belonged to others, this basement belonged solely to them.

The Babes were alone (together) in this place of gestation where they could get use to their instruments and each other. It was a completely new dynamic from the earlier version of the band, so much that there was discussion of rebaptizing the trio Swamp Pussy, but decided to use that for a song title and stick with the original moniker.[29]

They found they played off of each other fantastically, and better yet, they got along.

"Michelle was really fun because she played with her fingers." Barbero remembers.

> Compatibility over skill was more important, because you could always learn and change, and in a way, we were always looking for someone who originally didn't know how to play and hadn't been in other bands because they would have their own way of doing it. If they just played in this band, then they were just bringing it over to us, and we wanted our own thing. So it was more important for us to get someone that we really liked, even if they couldn't play.[30]

One way of teaching themselves how to play and write songs together were by spitballing sounds via the vocabulary of their musical influences. Each woman brought an eclectic set of tastes to the table. Barbero was mostly inspired by her favorite punk bands, but she also drew upon her New York glam rock days. While she cites that listening to Scottish band The Scars gave her a feel for drumming, she has also stated that Alice Cooper's "Halo of Flies" was the gateway song that made her want to drum.[31] While she wouldn't act on that until many year later, she would always watch the drummers in her favorite bands:

> There were a lot of locals that I really loved and observed for many years, one being Tony Pucchi from Man Sized

Action . . . he used a lot of high toms . . . [and] Grant Hart [Husker Dü], was a big influence because I played barefoot and he always played barefoot, and I always thought that was the way you do it.[32]

Barbero's favorite band at the time, The Minutemen, gave her and Bjelland the idea to restructure the band into a trio.[33]

Barbero was also impressed with the vocalizations of Kat Arthur in the L.A. punk band, Legal Weapon: "It just had this drive that I really loved, not that I wanted to sound like them, but that, I don't want no pussyfoot kind of band."[34]

Tough chicks were the patron saints of the basement practices. Leon's love of new wave held a special appreciation for the women in bands like X, Siouxsie and the Banshees, Bow Wow Wow, The Fall, The Talking Heads, as well as Legal Weapon and The Cramps.[35] Patti Smith was the band's patron Goddess.

Bjelland loved the emotional range and vulnerability of Billie Holiday, but in regard to vocals she also wasn't pussyfooting around, and preferred the more experimental and extreme: "You know who I really thought was cool though, was Nina Hagen, because of her range. I always thought, 'Man, if I could do that, that would be hot!' So, she kind of inspired me as far as like, 'You can sing!'"[36]

Nina Hagen was born and raised in East Berlin and brought an interesting marriage of old-world theatrics and cold war trauma and was able to translate it into something unique within US and UK new-wave and punk performances in the early 1980s. She is most known in the United States for

Nunsexmonkrock (1982), and if this was what Bjelland was vibing on, it all makes sense. Hagen was trained in opera, and exploited those skills into an extraterrestrial range that goes from chirping to yodeling, Gollum-esque gurgles and hisses, orgiastic snorts and grunts—all to erupt into perfect operatic scales. It's crazy shit; I can see exactly how she inspired Bjelland.

Hagen's performances are strange, confronting, burlesque, and completely grotesque. Notions of femininity so often reinforced within formal avenues like opera and jazz are completely fragmented and shattered. She seems like a woman possessed, or possibly body snatched—an intergalactic alien camouflaged within the glamour of a gothic cabaret singer—and her complete abandon to this passion reminds me of the same sense of possession Bjelland projected in her performances, especially those around 1991 and 1992.

Bjelland wasn't interested in just belting out lyrics, as punk so often did in the 1970s and 1980s. She wanted to create a new sonic experience. While she saw women breaking narratives within bands like Frightwig and Wendy O Williams of The Plasmatics, they perhaps lacked the insane sense of vocal theatricality that she saw Hagen bringing to the table. While doing press for *Fontanelle* in 1992, she told the *Los Angeles Times*:

> It *should* be extreme. It should sound like nothing that you've heard before. That's my intention. . . . Like my singing, all I try to do is I just push myself into things where I think I can't reach notes and stuff. Sometimes it

sounds really ridiculous, but then you just kind of work on it. Just I always like experimental stuff.[37]

Back in the basement, Bjelland knew how to play guitar, but she was having to teach herself how to sing, and it was a musical evolution that she would work on for the rest of her career with the band.

The influence rings clearest on *Fontanelle*, but Bjelland pushed herself to experiment with her own range from 1986 onwards. On *Spanking Machine*, she explored its potential in songs like "Dust Cake Boy," "Spit to See the Shine," and "Fork Down Throat." Within these songs she experiments with dramatic punctuation and scatting in growls and howls. *To Mother* becomes more chaotic and exhibits the band's more hypnotic trademark auditory tornado sound. In "Map Pilot," Bjelland gives a rabid performance of agitation that begins immediately with bite and backs down with sweet siren croons only to relapse into gnashing teeth and spit. "Laugh My Head Off" exhibits disdain as phonation.

You can really hear her range in the Babes' *Peel Sessions*, where the variations in her singing and screaming and everything in between are more improvisational. Bjelland's versatility isn't always perfectly captured on tape. It's in the live shows that you can see how her style evolves and how she learns to inflect drama into her delivery. But as far as recorded performances go, the most masterful showcase of Bjelland's range is found on *Fontanelle's* "Mother." It uses switching perspectives and a Pentecostal-like possession where Bjelland shrieks and scats in tongues.

"When you scream like that, it's just like you're just letting yourself go." Bjelland told documentarian Lisa Rose Apramian. "Like you just go up into your head and whatever comes out comes out . . . it's like you just let something else take over."[38]

Down in the basement, the Babes utilized their diverse tastes to experiment with sounds, but they never once aspired to replicate something someone else did, nor would they ever try to compete against other artists. They took inspiration from the music they loved, but never allowed themselves to become overly influenced by it. Despite admiring a band for this and another performer for that, the overall objective was to create something no one had ever heard before. And in the safety of the basement, they did.

They had no idea that once the trio left their own private underworld that what they were doing would catch the attention of an entire zeitgeist.

Plate 2
Knifesliding

First Songs

Like much of the band's history, some uncertainty surrounds what the first Babes in Toyland song may have been. In a *Phawker* interview from 2015, Bjelland recalls: "'Spit to See the Shine' was the first song we ever wrote . . . or no, it was: 'Jungle Tramp'. [*Sic*] 'Spit To See The Shine' was a close second because it was simple chords."[1] However, in Leon's account of her first practice, she portrays Bjelland teaching her how to play the bass-line to "Spit to See the Shine."[2]

I think the reason for the confusion is they both were first, in a sense. Since Bjelland upcycled riffs from her earlier bands, it seems reasonable to think "Spit to See the Shine" and "Catatonic" were offered as quick songs to practice and build upon in the earlier incarnations of the Babes. It was probably the first song that Barbero and Bjelland collaborated on, but as far as the first complete effort between Leon, Barbero, and Bjelland goes, "Jungle Train" was probably the prototype for all the other songs to come.

"Kat usually brings a song structure to practice, the foundation." Leon writes. "I find notes that match of melodies to complement the chords. Sometimes Lori starts with a heavy drumbeat, the rhythm powerful, simple, complete."[3]

"Jungle Train" is perfect for building a sound together. While it has lyrics on *Fontanelle*, its origins were purely instrumental. A jam song, it doesn't aim to be thematically whole. It exists almost like a Dada Sound Poem, where there are no words—just the beginning semblances of unique resonances—and it is distinctly different every time it is performed. In fact, it's a pretty good gauge of how quickly the band coheres together when you see it performed in some of the earlier live shows available on YouTube. In the Cabooze 1988[4] footage, there are no lyrics at all, just jamming.

In this performance, you can hear the distinct sonic personalities of each person. As they continue to tune into each other, "Jungle Train" becomes the band's individuation anthem. You can see how much mileage Barbero can get out of one Tom drum. With the exception of a cymbal, it's the sole generator of the jam's beat. You can see Leon exploring and feeling into different fingerings, while Bjelland, standing closer to the amps, away from the mic, lets her Rickenbacker wail.

Six months later at the October 29, 1988,[5] Uptown show, Barbero drums faster, but Bjelland's guitar meanders with frequent, exploratory pauses of feedback and distortion. Leon's riff is more confident—her notes keep the rhythmic chaos bound within their melodic mire. They never stick to the same formula, they always come back to the core.

First Shows

"First one was in a basement underneath a convenience store on Chicago Avenue." Barbero remembers. "I think it was pretty simple and easy for us to do because it was in a basement and that's where we had been rehearsing, so it was comfortable and familiar to us rather than a stage somewhere—some venue. It was a basement, just like rehearsal."[6]

Accounts assess the first show as a cacophonous but unforgettable moment within the Minneapolis music scene. Terri Sutton, the *City Pages* pioneering feminist music critic and early supporter of the band, recalled: "Their sound was peeling paint off the wall, but they had this tremendous energy that somehow redeemed how bad they were. . . . You could tell that these women were doing a brave and dangerous thing to just get up there and play."[7]

There is no record of the exact date, but it was probably not far from their 7th Street Entry debut on June 19, 1987.[8] No footage has surfaced of any 1987 shows, but you can get a sense of what Sutton meant through the two previously mentioned concerts from 1988. These early performances show the Babes experimenting with their sound and each other. They seem stiff; each stand in their own corners of the stage, overly focused on their instruments.

These early shows demonstrate how the women used the stage to hone in on their skills. Each gig wasn't just an opportunity to perform, but to practice and continue the fun. They didn't wait for perfection and plunged right in. By being unafraid of mistakes, they cultivated a healthy relationship with experimentation, which allowed their sound to evolve organically over numerous practices, performances, and recording sessions. But despite this, the polished Babes were never too far off from their raw early days. And I think this was because they never went in for fancy productions of their recordings, relying on as few takes to stay as authentic to their live sound as possible on reel. But because Bjelland varies her presentation in each performance, it's actually rewarding to listen to the same sets again and again because of her experimental improvisations.

In "Fake Fur Condoms," at the Cabooze, for example, Bjelland makes noises over the mostly instrumental early version of this song. She experiments with vocal punctuations structuring a seemingly spontaneous, screaming vocabulary that she will become famous for.

The band took turns for a while singing, an extension of their matrilineal ethos of equal and valuable players within the band. Most songs were sung by Bjelland, but Barbero would break up the set with her sultry, bluesy spoken word contralto—in these shows it's "You Know That Guy" and "Dogg." This pattern would also be honored on all of their albums.

Not everything they played with worked. While Leon is never featured singing lead vocals on any of the albums, she did sing one song, "Milk Pond," at the 1988 Cabooze Show. It's a fractured song that wants to keep it together through a punk dominance, but the various pieces refuse to align. This song was quickly dropped from their sets, and the singing left to Bjelland and Barbero.

In between these two shows, which were about six months apart, you also get a sense of how fast they were writing songs. By April 14, 1988, the earliest show with available footage, they played a set consisting of eleven songs:

Knife Song
Flesh Crawl
Boto (w)rap
Milk Pond
Jungle Train
Fake Fur Condom
Instrumenstrual
You Know That Guy
Never
Swamp Pussy
Fork Down Throat

By October 29, 1988, when the band played the Uptown Bar in Minneapolis they had added six more songs to their repertoire:

Arriba
You're Right
He's My Thing
Short Song
Dogg
Map Pilot

By 1989, they are tight and owning the stage at 7th Avenue Entry—the Mecca that brought the girls together. Leon is in full charge of her bass and gives over to its power, following its lead in a dance only they know, whereas before she would stand stiffly and not face the audience. They all are open now, in sync, and rocking out in tandem ecstasy. As Leon describes it, what they were beginning to generate on stage was something unique and magical: "The three of us create heavenly heat. . . . All that we love channels above us as we play. A trio of ghostly vapors tangling together, rising."[9]

Most of the songs that are on *Spanking Machine* (1990) and *To Mother* (1991) begin to appear, which unlocks the potential for Bjelland to begin experimenting with her vocal ranges:

House
Pain in My Heart
Dirty
Lashes
Vomit Heart
Dust Cake Boy
Laugh My Head Off

By summer of 1989, all of the songs that would be on their first LP, *Spanking Machine*, have been written. Within a year, they had begun to generate an enthusiastic buzz and following, and 1989 presented them with the opportunity to bust out of Minneapolis and take Babes in Toyland on the road. They were playing in the most iconic and hottest venues in the punk scene at the time thanks to Barbero's vast network:

The thing was that bands always stayed at my house that were on tour and I got to know tons of bands, and I had a record label, and I just got to know everybody . . . so the next thing I knew is, like, we started playing and this band [Die Kruezen] . . . were going on tour and they asked us if we wanted to go on tour . . . . And it was before White Zombie got big and they were the middle slot, and that was our first tour.[10]

To start touring, the band bought a used white van, christened it "Vanna White,": "And then we went out with the Cows from Minneapolis," Barbero recalled. "And that was really super fun, and it just kind of started going from there. We did so many tours—Dinosaur, Jr., Faith No More, Lollapolloza, Sonic Youth . . . that was the greatest, all of them were great . . . I miss it a lot because I miss traveling and I loved playing."[11] For ten years on, Babes in Toyland toured ten months out of the year. For Leon, who joined the band when she was seventeen, that consisted of four years of her early adult life. She basically grew up on the road, and sometimes found their skyrocketing ascent through the scene exhausting: "We always were able to get shows, or sometimes it was, like, too many shows. You know what I mean? Like, it's maybe not good to play once a week. You want it to be special when you have a show."[12]

First Recordings

The Babes released their first single, "Dust Cake Boy/Spit to See the Shine," in 1989 through Minneapolis's Treehouse records. "He [label owner Mark Trehus] just came to us and said, '*Hey, do you wanna do a single?*,' *a*nd I thought, sure!" Bjelland recounted. "He liked us. We've sold the most singles on Treehouse of all his bands so far."[13]

This was due to the band's relentless promotion via their touring as well as a bit of luck when it landed on John Peel's desk in England: "We get letters from England and Spain, that's where most of the ordering of the record and the fan mail comes from. I guess they played us on the [John] *Peel Sessions*."[14]

It was recorded sometime in October 1988 at Technisound Studio by Brian Paulson. Paulson was a long-time friend of the band, and a great ally during the *Fontanelle* days: "I think we recorded that at this weird little 8-track studio in South Minneapolis, if I remember correctly. Kind of a quick and dirty thing, like in an afternoon probably."[15]

The Babes would find quick and dirty was how they liked their studio session. The positive experience they had at Technisound Studio with Paulson would set the precedence for how they would always prefer to record: together in the studio and knocking out the tracks as though they were playing live. This would be how they would record their following albums up until *Fontanelle*, all "down in one or two takes," according to Leon.[16]

Immensely lo-fi and fuzzy, all of the instruments melt together within Bjelland's scorn, which sounds like its reverberating through a soup can. Even so, her words are clear.

"Dust Cake Boy" is antithesis to the Torch songs women are expected to sing about their lovers. Love is present, but it's shackling rather than sublime. It's raunchy, caked in dirt and bodily fluids, and is both jarring and relatable in its beatific grime.

It creates an archetype—it defines that kind of greasy-haired Adonis who is Toxicity embodied, but of whom you just can't get enough, despite how bad they are for you. We've all known a Dust Cake Boy (or Girl!):

"'Dust Cake' was based on a real life scenario." Bjelland explained in 2015. "I met someone from Annapolis that I liked a lot. His name is Billy . . . that's why I say 'Indian Billy simple sin,' in there. I've actually talked to him since then. We had this thing and it's continual inspiration."[17]

While Bjelland remembers Billy fondly, Leon alludes to him as nothing but bad news—the man who turned Bjelland onto smack, and relapses her throughout the years every time he reappears.[18] This perhaps explains the intro where Bjelland comes in wailing to shoot—it could be cupid, a challenge, or a dare to shoot-up—but the suggestion revs up the bad romance whirlwind that progresses throughout verses. Lovesick and smack-sick twin in spirals throughout the whole song. When she describes Indian Billy and the effects he has on her, it isn't soft caresses but soft gravel—and the friction of their union leaves her ill.

The chorus is jam-packed with Bjelland's trademark double entendres. The "hole" she laments could be metaphysical, but also physical, either perhaps through coitus or track marks—both needing to be filled by something elusive and fleeting like love or salvation. Both the abscess and absence is tied to her soul, to her heart—and it captures perfectly the confused emotions found in a passionately toxic romance. In either image a weary, passive expression usually heard as a sighing lament becomes reclaimed as brute and menacing rage.

This innocent eruption into the taboo of female violence is Bjelland and the Babes' aesthetic signature. It would become more fully realized around *Fontanelle*, but is evident and perfected in this particular recording. The Treehouse single is so raw, that you get a sense of what an encounter with the Babes was like during these days, when access was limited to only live shows: "I can't think of anything as powerful as what the Babes were putting out there at that time." Paulson recalled. "Sure we had Têtes Noires and we had Frightwig and what not, but there was something about the raw power of what Bjelland put out, there wasn't anything like that at the time. It was terrifying—it made you stop and think."[19]

The Babes' aesthetics would eventually evolve from that raw musical power and into a more visual confrontation with the infantilization of the female experience, but those visual aspects aren't lent to "Dust Cake Boy's" packaging and would not begin to emerge until the release of their first album, *Spanking Machine*. On both sides, the single features Brad Miller's unassuming band portraits. The only connection his images have with their overall branding is that the women look happy and peaceful, which obviously contradicts the violence and anger of the songs within the sleeve.

"Dust Cake Boy" received a lot of play on the college radio circuit, and it exposed them to listeners beyond the Twin Cities' scenes. It began to generate heat as well as an avidly growing fan base that became increasing more female. This audience would connect with the band so intensely that it would spur them on to start their own bands: "They were just so powerful and almost kind of intimidating," Selby Tigers and Pink Mink's Arzu Gokcen recalled in 2015. "It was like there was no vulnerability to them at all. That sound they would make would just hit you so hard, but it was only three of them and it wasn't anything too complex. I thought, 'If they can do that, I can do it, too.'"[20]

Reciprocal Recording Studio Sessions

Another first for the band in 1989 was signing with Twin/Tone Records, who flew the band out to Seattle's Reciprocal Recording Studios to record their full-length debut with Jack Endino: "There were five days booked, and the mission was to record the album plus a Sub Pop single plus one song for a *Teriyaki Asthma* comp single for C/Z Records. Sub Pop actually paid for one of the studio days, Twin Tone paid for the rest." "House" and "Arriba" would make up the Sub Pop Singles Club 7-inch, and "Flesh Crawl" the C/Z contribution.

Out of these three songs, "House" is the most conceptual, playing on the childhood game of heterosexual, nuclear family mores. In Bjelland's version, the adult realization of this game is neither idealistic nor innocent, and displays a darker reality that the "playing house" idea avoids—domestic abuse. Within the verses, the narrator accounts of all injuries sustained at her boyfriend's house, only to then backpedal into declarations of love. The pain and excuses are dizzying, reinforced by a bright, rockabilly groove orchestrating the confusion. It all comes to a halt when Bjelland asks if this is what love feels like?

The chorus breaks from its frenzied klutziness to slow in to a drunken crawl. The mood has gone from victim to vigilante—from passive to aggressive—from denial to survival. In a heart-stopping vocal fry growl, Bjelland flips an all-to-familiar refrain to domestic violence survivors: "Just try and shut my mouth."

The attempts to keep women silent and the struggle to have our stories heard are embodied within this dynamic reversal. Even though Bjelland is depicting a microcosmic example of her experience, one that unfortunately so many others identify with at that same level, macrocosmically that chorus challenges everything the patriarchy has tried to throw at us: "Why don't you shut your mouth, before I shut it for you." It's a threat that many women who are trapped within the realities of playing house have heard countless time before. Bjelland isn't playing these games anymore. She shuts her lover up and shuts down his base attempt at patriarchal dominance.

It's an empowering song, because the chorus performs a simple rebellion—it encourages women to speak up, not shut up.

First Album

Babes recorded *Spanking Machine* over five days, each track done within a few takes. Jack Endino designed Reciprocal Recording Studios to capture bands at their best, by simulating a live show in an open room with all needed equipment and gear. This allowed the band to play together as though they were on stage, and live was always the Babes' best side. They were thrilled to find that they and Endino were on the same page, and laying down the tracks was easy as all agreed to leave in mistakes, like at the end of "He's My Thing" where Leon is off on the last note.[21]

"They knew what they wanted exactly," Jack Endino recalled, "and they were pretty well prepared. The sessions went very smoothly, with no problems that I remember."[22] It was recorded and mixed on a one-inch 16-track machine at 15 IPS. There were "no tricks. Just mixing things correctly and giving them a good headphone mix."[23]

While each band member claimed to not be perfectionists, I don't actually believe that was true for Bjelland. The other members of the band never seemed to care much about the production side of making an album, but Bjelland would become interested in the infinite possibilities and improvements of sound engineering. Leon cites Bjelland staying up late with Endino to help with the mixing while the other women went out.[24] This would give her the vocabulary she needed to communicate studio visions in the future with *Fontanelle*.[25]

Released April 16, 1990, *Spanking Machine* was an indie success. It received rave notice in *Entertainment Weekly*,[26] and sold about 50,000 units all told, both happenings a huge feat for a band's debut from an indie label.[27] It also charted on the UK Indie Charts thanks to John Peel's enthusiasm. While he had already been impressed with the Babes with "Dust Cake Boy," fell in love with them when he heard "House," and gave it copious air play alongside *Spanking Machine*, which he named his favorite album of 1990. He could not get enough, and soon neither could his listeners.

European Debut

Spanking Machine was impressing a lot of people, and it especially impressed Sonic Youth's Thurston Moore, who asked the Babes to support them on their *Goo* European tour that summer. This also allowed them to meet their growing fan base abroad, including a live session for John Peel and recording their second Twin/Tone release, *To Mother*, with John Loder at Southern Studios. It was a short, two-day affair, and it would be released summer 1991. It would enter the UK Indie Chart at number 1 and remain there for ten weeks.[28]

"On that tour, nothing stood in their way." Moore observed in an *NME* celebration. "They were very tough; they were not a neat band in any sense of the word—they were badasses."[29] The women were become amazing performers. Leon would bang her bass, Barbero would commune with her drums, and Bjelland explored various ways to bend her Rickenbacker, including a pretty harmful technique: "I do this thing called a Knifeslide," Bjelland explained to Liz Evans. "Where I bend my guitar and it makes this really cool noise. I learned it from my first boyfriend who had a Flying V. I have bruises all over my hips and stomach from hitting my guitar and bending it!"[30] These incorporations of bending would lend a blues and jazz vibe to the overall noise of shredding and power chords. On "Magick Flute," she became legend for using knives as guitar slides, witnessed by Moore: "I remember watching them in Germany and . . . Kat Bjelland dropped to her knees, pulled out a butter knife and played slide guitar with it. The audience were stunned, but I just thought to myself, 'This is as good as it gets.'"[31]

When The Babes returned home, they were bona fide rock stars. They were checking off all the boxes: they were playing high-profiled shows alongside their friends and heroes; their songwriting grew more complex as they became better and tighter musicians; and they had singles that were in constant rotation at college radio and abroad and a fresh debut album that was actually selling and generating buzz.

They felt like they had made it: "'Success' to us, in Minneapolis, meant playing the main room at First Avenue or a sold-out show on a Saturday night at the Uptown bar. And we did that!" Leon recalled.

> There were US shows we would have liked a bigger crowd, or enough money for hotel rooms, but I don't ever remember feeling like we hadn't achieved what we set out to achieve, or that our trajectory was not good enough. However, we definitely liked how it felt to be successful in Europe and tour more comfortably, so we spent more time there.[32]

They couldn't have asked for more, but as they continued touring, and their music became widely played and distributed, the Babes would begin to realize they were becoming bigger than they ever could imagine.

Anterior Fontanelle

All you need to start a fire is a flame. Although Babes in Toyland would deny it, they were a major spark that fueled third-wave feminism.

"Everyone wants us to shoulder this . . . feminist girl/slut cause. I don't know what it is . . . bad girl cause?" Bjelland lamented in 1993. "And the main reason I wanted to get in a band was to do music. I didn't realize it entailed all this political stuff."[1] This quote came shortly after *Fontanelle*'s release, and was a response to the onslaught of media coverage that tried to apply the politics of riot grrrl to any and every band that had a "girl" in it. Because of *Fontanelle*'s timing, it would be released in the mainstream at a moment that would make it seem like Babes in Toyland came after riot grrrl rather than before. As such, the band suddenly found themselves thrusted into a political discussion they didn't want to be involved in. Even in 2021, they resist the categorizations as Barbero makes clear:

> People can see us, watch us, perceive what they want to and think what they want to, but we didn't go out there standing on stage going "Equal rights!" We were just

women in a band, you know, just doing the same thing dudes do but have different organs. We worked harder. Women have to sometimes work harder than men to get the same, but I would never say that we were a feminist band or a women's activist band, we never preached anything, you know, we were just a punk rock band who toured and had fun.[2]

They didn't need to preach because all of the testimony was in their music and performance.

Whether they intended to or not, the Babes began to be seen somewhat politically simply because their willingness to confront gender norm contradictions was countercultural. These were women who "dropped" out of the normal trajectory of women in their twenties to live on the edge. Countless men were doing this, but they didn't have as much to lose as women did at the time—or they thought they did. So to see women do this, and do it righteously and with such artistry, created a new kind of paradigm.

The Babes were the embodiment of punk rock's anti-establishment ethos. They were women who needed no authority or validation, and certainly weren't sitting around waiting for permission to live their lives. Most of all, they rebutted the fetishization of weak women and demonstrated that you can be strong and assertive without sacrificing your femininity. As Bjelland told Lisa Rose Apramian in *Not Bad for a Girl*: "I don't feel helpless or anything. I don't feel like I have to be like 'I'm a female, and I can do this if I want to!' Of course I can. I already know that. I never thought being female hurt anything. If anything, it helped."[3]

This impact began to take hold during 1990, as their relentless touring promoting *Spanking Machine* exposed them to more audiences. They were beginning to get fans, many of whom were now women: "When we started out playing, it used to be like 75% men, 25% women . . . and now it's like 50/50, and the women get right up in front, which you never use to see until about a year and a half ago."[4] Within these audiences were soon-to-be trailblazers who would take the personal rage they saw performed within the Babes and transmute it into their own radical forms of expression.

Babes Catching the Waves

Third-wave feminism's rise is said to have begun alongside the formation of Bikini Kill and the resulting riot grrrl movement, but what is little discussed about this is Babes in Toyland's role in stoking this fire. Sometime in the spring of 1990,[5] right around *Spanking Machine*'s release, Babes in Toyland played a house show in the middle of the woods in Olympia. Most of the attendees were students at Evergreen State College, a hot bed of student feminist activism and discourse, and among them were Kathleen Hannah, Tobi Vail, and Kathi Wilcox. While the show was a revelation to them, the rest of the audience began to dismiss the Babes for various reasons: "I was like, wow!" Hannah remembered. "You really can have it all! You can make this amazing music which was about how beautiful anger can be to me. I'd never heard anything like it." The crowd moved outside to a bonfire to discuss what on Earth they had just seen. Hannah stood alongside Vail and Wilcox. Like, Hannah, they felt they had just had a once-in-a-lifetime experience, and were all dumbfounded that everyone else thought the band was awful.[6]

People debated the performance quite extensively—they questioned whether the Babes knew how to play their instruments, questioned their talent in contrast to their attractiveness, and, overall, dismissed them as an all-girl novelty: "People were just plain confused by the greatness they'd experienced, it was too new, too different and too damn good to have come out of three girls."[7] Hanna, Vail, and Wilcox bonded over their agreement that this had been the best and most pivotal show they'd ever witnessed, and that the crowd's dismissal of the Babes for being "too pretty" completely avoided what the band had achieved: "They didn't have to hide the fact that they were women to play this totally intense music; the combination of the femininity with the strength in the music in saying that femininity and strength weren't the opposite of each other. It was a really intense experience."[8] Hannah, Vail, and Wilcox formed Bikini Kill shortly thereafter.

The Scream of the Medusa

Hannah's experience reveals so many aspects to Babes in Toyland's story that needs healing. It's widely known they were a polarizing band, but the why is barely discussed. Most people point to the screaming, but Bjelland's caterwauling was just the cathartic valve to an overall aesthetic that confronted the many contradictions of female experience unresolved by second-wave feminism. For as many people that it made uncomfortable, there were as many that it empowered.

White Lung's Mish Way was immediately impressed with Babes in Toyland when she first heard them. "When she shrieked the word 'motherfucker,' I felt it in my whole body." she wrote for *Talkhouse* in 2013. Way shared a love of music with her brother. They both adored Led Zeppelin and Robert Plant's abandoned wailing. When it came to Babes in Toyland, however, she found he couldn't stomach it: "My brother hated it because it made him uncomfortable. Women are not supposed to be lions. We're supposed to be lambs, and lambs do not scream 'motherfucker' while tearing open a Rickenbacker like a beast ripping the feathers off its prey."[9]

Way was right. Up until Babes in Toyland—women were supposed to be lambs who were herded and tended, gentle and docile. But Bjelland's screaming isn't about submission, but confrontation. In doing so, she gave space to the sort of emotional exhibition that had only been allowed for male entertainers. In fact, the only time entertainment finds the female scream acceptable is when its expression stems from victimization. When a woman screams, it is assumed violence is being done against her—but within Babes in Toyland, the implied violence is deflected and inflicted back. This was a woman—three women, in fact—who refused to be herded and led to slaughter.

"It's almost a theme in our lyrics I've noticed sometimes." Maureen Herman noted in a promo interview for *Painkillers*.

"It's just kind of like an independent attitude. Kind of take a stand even though you've been told not to. . . . Just kind of like an aggressive way of living."[10]

Aggression and violence were masculine purview, and by embracing them the Babes reinvented their feminine presentation from places of victimization and vulnerability into testimony and strength. This was a message many young girls during the late 1980s and early 1990s were missing in their lives, and once they encountered it— via the stage or on tape—it was life changing. For many, like music critic Jessica Hopper, Bjelland's voice was permission to make one's self heard: "Her scream was pure possibility."[11]

Although they always maintained their music was personal, and not political, they developed a unique aesthetic that constantly confronted and contradicted what it meant to be feminine, which usually meant a silencing akin to what Bjelland experienced: "I was told to shut-up a lot. I wasn't allowed to speak that much. . . . I was really confined to how I explained myself and stuff, and if I did, it was the wrong answer."[12]

Crazy Old Dolls

Spanking Machine was not only the band's full-length debut, but the premier of what would become their overlying aesthetic flipping girlhood nostalgia against the harsher truths of female violence and objectification. Lori chose the name *Spanking Machine* from a childhood memory of a birthday party game where everyone lined up to spank the birthday girl as she passed them.[13] It's a very interesting Freudian image—funny and cute as a child, but when you apply hindsight and adult context, it begins to take on sexual associations of fetish. This, aligned with the rest of the album's visual presentation, connotes a sense of innocence and play distorted by an insidious violence driven by the male gaze.

Spanking Machine's cover[14] presents the band members buried under hundreds of vintage baby dolls. They almost blend in with the doll pit, but their direct gaze into the camera asserts a jarring disassociation with their bodies from that of the dolls. To Generation X, these particular toys would have been a direct gender identifier for little girls, and like many childhood games, were a grooming function for their adult roles as mother and wife. The expectation was that little girls would learn to care and nurture their dolls like real-life babies. But the reality was that as children get bored or mature, these tokens of care would begin to have limbs or heads pop off or become so filthy they are thrown away.

The dolls depicted in *Spanking Machine* and its following promotions were all vintage shop finds. Obviously neglected and discarded, they played with the idea of the disposability of the female body and the expectation of the feminine to be contained within the idealized notions of girlhood. The Babes' presence among this dusty nostalgic pit, paired with the innuendo of the album's title, presents a contradiction women were having to face—that society wanted little girls to develop in a certain way, and if they couldn't conform, or worse complained, then they easily could be destroyed and thrown away like an old rag doll.

These motifs are further developed in the album's only video single, "He's My Thing." Made by Phil Harder and Mike Etoll, it is an interesting stop-motion animation following the adventures of a Bjelland-eque doll. Naked, with wide eyes and matted blonde hair, she makes a deal with a devil that makes her ensnare and sever another baby doll's leg as an offering. He rewards her by setting her on fire. The video ends with her hair singed, her face melted, and only her two coal-black eyes staring blankly at the viewer. It's a video that seems disarmingly sweet until the doll has an axe, and it disintegrates naturally into a violence that is reminiscent of how little boys played with their GI Joe figurines rather than little girls in a playtime nursery. In other words, it takes something soft and overtly feminine and reveals that a capacity for violence (often attributed to the masculine) lies beneath.

It's an immensely clever cinematic translation of the song. "He's My Thing" flips the male gaze and sense of possessiveness on its head and places it in the power of the women. It mimics the same sort of machismo expected of two men fighting over one woman, but these women are tugging at the eponymous "Thing" boyfriend like a stretch doll. It's aggressive, menacing, and unsentimental. It certainly gives new meaning to what a "torch song" can be about.

The doll metaphor wasn't limited only to commentary on the male gaze and the female body, but also to the broken promises of childhood innocence. The 1990s were a time when many artists were speaking out about how fractured and awful their childhoods were. They were the first generation widely affected by divorce, and overall acknowledged that the nuclear American suburban life could be more nightmare than dream. While Bjelland would often shy away from being blatant about what happened to her, it is well documented that she lived a harsh life suffering abuse and misery as a child.[15] She did not have an idyllic childhood by any means, and it thematically informs a great deal of her lyrical subjects. *Spanking Machine*, then, is her first exhibit of these meditations, and is an album full of unanswered questions with five out of the eleven songs on the album asking "Why" to off-screen antagonists.

"Pain in my Heart" is the epitome of this criss-crossing of childhood helplessness with adult consequence. This is a heartbreaking song written in Bjelland's trademark fragmentary style (discussed further later on). It begins as a single long question and asks someone why they left her. Perhaps because of Bjelland's experiences, I've always assumed this someone was her mother because she goes on to explain that she was left while still inside of this person. Of course, Bjelland's mother left her when she was three years old, and not in the womb—but it certainly connotes abandonment at an early stage of development, or that the mother never wanted the child within her to begin with. It's a haunting refrain with many possibilities bleeding into the album's overall themes of discarded dolls and transforming them into unwanted children. This question in "Pain in My Heart" begets more questions, all of which get swept up in a stream-of-consciousness spiral that keeps spinning and spinning further away from resolution or answers and the song ends where it began by asking the eternally unanswerable "Why?"

While "Pain in my Heart" is more of an internal monologue of remembering past childhood trauma, other songs in *Spanking Machine* call upon the doll motif much more heavily to reveal that the sweet, soft exterior presented by the album cover and Bjelland's fairy-like handwritten font is rock hard inside. Songs like "Lashes" are immensely violent and nightmarish. Every verb connotes pain and the chorus focuses on the ruptures of structures reinforced by seemingly innocent childhood games like "House." The second stanza depicts children grown out of their fantasy and into miserable adults still trying to keep up the charade of romantic bliss. The female of course, is named Baby, and is so disassociated from what her life has become that by the end of the last stanza she confesses she feels pointless like "a crazy old doll."

"Vomit Heart" is another song with dolls, and uses that motif to draw parallels between innocent violence acted out in childhood and the way those practices carry through into sexual dynamics. We always think of children playing nicely with their toys, but if anyone remembers their childhood correctly, it was also an avenue to explore violence without repercussions. You can treat dolls abhorrently and there are no consequences. To treat something like an object is to do whatever you want with it and have no shame or repercussions. Bjelland depicts the decapitations and limb-severing of dolls as metaphors to how a romance is tearing her apart, and how she feels so easily discardable and destroyed.

Ripe

Their next album, *To Mother*, adds another aesthetic and existential layer to the Babes' aesthetic explorations. It is an auditory tornado filled with childhood cant fragmented with adult angst. The cover features a literal babe in all of her innocence. The child is Bjelland's biological mother, Lynne, who died while the Babes were in London recording the EP at Southern Studios. To honor her, the Babes agreed to run the cover image along with childhood photos of each band-member inside.[16] "It was like a tribute to her." Bjelland told Liz Evans in 1994. "She was really cool, I wish I had got to know her a lot better, but she got cancer."[17]

It sounds like, that despite what happened to Bjelland when she was young, she was able to stay in touch with her mother throughout her life and come to understand her actions. While we currently have no context of what it took for Bjelland to forgive and forget her abandonment, I can't help but wonder if, as Bjelland grew older, part of it was an understanding about what motherhood is versus what we are told it means.

One of the core wounds of trying to redefine womanhood is confronting the right or the rejection of becoming a mother. It is assumed, even today, that all little girls want to grow up to have babies. A self-fulfilling career or other life interests are all seen as supplementary to the fulfillment of the female biological imperative. And if they are childless, then they are selfish and unfulfilled.

But for as many men who don't want to be fathers, there are as many women who don't want to be mothers. In a situation of conception, the woman has less choice and more stigma and cannot reject the role and move through life unpunished as easily as a man can. In Lynne Bjelland's time, in 1963, she had very little choice when pregnant. But it is obvious, that after having Bjelland the motherly instinct didn't kick in. When Bjelland got sick at three years old, it was too much for Lynne, who was "a poor hippie in San Francisco and couldn't take care of me."[18] She did what a lot of women have probably wanted to do, she left.

And so the cover image is not only a eulogy, but also another form of confrontation. At the age of three, in her best dress and shoes, little Lynne Higginbotham has no notion of what the realities of her girlhood will become when she grows up into the woman Lynne Bjelland. And while the women whom the little girls inside the album sleeve grow up to lead much different lives, they too have no idea what is expected of them or what they might or might not become. These portraits are blank slates whose bodies are *not yet* confined or defined by their sexual function or societal roles.

We can have some sympathy for Lynne Bjelland's situation, but it still doesn't erase the fact that her actions affected and damaged her daughter for a really long time. Lyle Bjelland soon remarried, and his new wife became Kat Bjelland's abuser throughout her childhood. This entire sequence of events was understandably traumatic, and not only did it appear as a major motif in *Spanking Machine*, but it will continue to be explored in *Fontanelle* at an even more sophisticated artistic level.

But around this time, Bjelland begins to continue these conversations through another visual avenue: her dress.

While discussions of Kinderwhore as a fashion movement have reduced costuming down to slip and baby doll dresses, bobby socks, and Mary Jane shoes, this wasn't exactly the look Bjelland would cultivate and become known for. Bjelland's vintage dresses harkened back specifically to her mother's era, be it from the 1930s and 1940s, when Lynne Bjelland was a child, or the early 1960s (the height of the Peter Pan collar) when she was a young mother. While other Kinderwhore pioneers like Garside and Love had their own takes and intent with this style—Bjelland's specifically always looked like a still from a Tennessee Williams or Alfred Hitchcock movie. Her dress didn't connote childhood so much as the fading ideas of femininity that would start to be taken back up as the "new feminine" within the 1980s media backlash. And as such, I believe the experiences she had with her biological mother inspired this aesthetic, but the message it shares is all Bjelland—the soft exterior only masks what's rock hard inside.

Blood

As mentioned before, the Babes were not a "pussyfooting kind of band." They explored the darkest and most taboo experiences of their lives through a feminine aesthetic that was undercut by the sort of aggression, violence, and grit expected of male performers. They weren't trying to be like men, or compete with them at their own games. They did, however, refuse to be denied the catharsis men are encouraged to enjoy through rage, angst, and aggression. In doing so, they presented a glimpse at the violence done to women without fetishizing victimization or seeming weak and conquered. They discussed taboo and difficult topics such as rape and domestic abuse—as they had personally experienced it—alongside more innocuous but nonetheless damaging perceptions about female perfection, addiction, and the complications of sisterhood.

"We're into confrontation," explained Bjelland to *Spin* magazine in 1992. "We write about getting sick of people who aren't honest. . . . Things that people can relate to."[19]

And they not only did it through voice but with their bodies.

In 1991, the Babes released a 7-inch single through Australian Insipid records for "Handsome and Gretel" and "Pearl." The single featured two images. The front featured Bjelland with a huge bow in her hair, bloodied and cut up in the back of a cop car. Her bruises were from a car accident while touring, but out of context, the image looks like she's been arrested for brawling. The other side showed a bruised Barbero with a swollen face and broken nose sustained from an abusive boyfriend.

"And I heard it was really polarizing for some people," Thurston Moore recalled in 2015. "Because it was like, 'Well, what does this say about women presenting themselves in music and entertainment?' It certainly was a bit of a wild statement—very independent, and I thought it was fascinating."[20]

It is fascinating because there are several contradictions to unpack in just two small images. First, domestic violence was hidden from the public back then. While violence against women was a popular trope in entertainment, these images would be for many the first real-life confrontation of what it actually looked like. It's not pretty, which brings us to the second reason people were repulsed.

Women in the music industry were supposed to be beautiful and flawless. By showing themselves at their worst and in this state of unwanted vulnerability, they confronted what society chose to see and ignore about many women's—even entertainers—imperfect realities. These weren't emotionless dolls; these were real people who suffered.

Through their word play, visual juxtapositions, and a willingness to perform personal wounds, they gave a missing and healing space to damaging female taboos that made young women suddenly feel not so alone with their secrets, confusion, and rage. Yes, their aesthetic was uncomfortable and aggressive, but so was the damaging mainstream, conservative conversation of what little girls should become versus what women actually became. It's a conversation that continues to today, making the much-needed catharsis Babes in Toyland provided then even more essential to our survival now.

Plate 3
An A&R Guy Walks into a Bar

On June 10, 1990, Babes in Toyland were offered representation by Warner Brother's A&R man, Tim Carr. Carr was a tastemaker famous for helping unlikely acts like the B-52s, Megadeath, and the Beastie Boys. Before he was an A&R rep, he was a journalist and involved in the art scene in both Minneapolis and New York City, allowing him to matchmake collaborations that bridged high art with underground music. In May, he had caught Babes at a nightcap show at The Pyramid Club in New York City and had been blown away: "I want music that makes me believe in God, in love, in passion . . . ." he wrote in his journal. "The closest I get is hearing the Babes purposefully play a lot of things wrong, on purpose."[1]

The band were surprised and skeptical by his interest, and they were not as convinced as Carr that their music could become radio-friendly. This wasn't from a lack of self-belief, but from the conviction that they would never allow their music to be morphed into pop-bizarro versions like The Go-Gos[2] and The Bangles,[3] who were transformed from aggressive, noisy, punk rock women to approachable, upbeat girl next door pop groups. For this reason alone, the Babes had never considered a major label, and as Bjelland depicts, told Carr several times where he could go: "I was like, 'I'm not going to change our sound, you f—. F— you! I don't want Bugs Bunny money.'" But Carr had no interest in transforming them; he wanted the world to hear them exactly as he had that first night. He vowed that if they signed with him, they'd get exposure to a larger audience without compromising their souls. It seems Carr was true to his words, as Bjelland confirmed in 2015: "They didn't change a thing."[4]

Even so, it took Carr over a year to both convince the band to sign while persuading Warner Brothers that there was money to be made by signing them. While he was an A&R representative for one of the largest major labels at the time, Carr's primary interest had always been to promote original art and artists. There would be no band he would fight harder for than the Babes. As a result, the Babes ended up having a much more positive and undramatic experience with the majors than a lot of their peers.

"I never felt victimized, no. Tim Carr . . . was our champion . . ." Bjelland responded to a query about how the music industry treated the band. "He basically was the middleman for talking to the bigwigs at . . . Warner Brothers. He was really good . . . . He was the one responsible for us getting signed. Which is odd—we were an odd band to be on a label. But he was really into music. I attribute a lot of our success to him."[5] Barbero, Leon, and Herman have all said the same when faced with similar inquiries. He would become "the fourth member of Babes in Toyland," according to Barbero. "He was just the most wonderful man . . . . I can't even struggle to think of a word against him, he was just the best."[6]

Carr's proposal was a transitional moment for the band. Not only did he see a commercial potential they had refused to believe was possible, but he also immediately recognized that their unique punk aesthetic could easily become elevated into high art. He saw the same terrain in their girlhood/womanhood visual notions as what was being explored in the New York feminist art scene, especially in the photographs of Cindy Sherman. He would eventually introduce the band to Sherman, and not only would she become a huge fan and collaborator during *Fontanelle*, but this would lend the band's aesthetic exploration even more feminist sheen.[7]

Everything Carr did for the Babes in the way of refining their aesthetics and coaxing their public presentation was never regarded as meddling from the band. Rather, they all felt he really understood their impulses and through his New York art connections, improved a vision the band had already been naturally gravitating towards for years. As Barbero recalled: "Tim didn't say this is how we're doing it. He'd just suggest stuff, and he was so fucking awesome that we never shunned him. We were never like 'Oh God, what kind of an idea is that.'"[8] And while the band rebuffed him the first time they met, they began to realize Carr's interest was sincere. By the summer of 1991, the fourth member of Babes in Toyland was inducted into the band when they agreed to sign with Carr and Reprise records.

Terms and Conditions

The Babes signed a deal for an advance of $200,000 in June 1991, and at this time no one could fathom a better kind of deal than this. These were pre-*Nevermind* numbers, and not too far off the mark of what their peers were given. For some context, Nirvana only got $287,000 when they signed with Geffen in April 1991.[9] In 1989, Geffen also picked up Sonic Youth for a five-album contract for $300,000.[10]

To get out of their four-album contract with Twin/Tone, they had to buy themselves out at $50,000. The Babes, themselves, were paid a total of $25,000 to be split equally between the three of them ($8,333 each). $18,000 went to the Producer's fee, and $27,000 would pay for the daily rental of two legendary studio spaces: Sorcerer's Studio and Pachyderm. This left a buffer of $98,000 to pay for services, like a cook, fees for sound engineer Brian Paulson and peacekeeper Tim Mac, and to cover the $30,000 that the extra days of reels and mixing would cost the band when the album went over schedule. The rest of it was surely gobbled up by personnel management fees and business writing fees, and certainly the prestigious services of their new power lawyer, Richard Grabel, who was paid $10,000.[11] Grabel's presence helped secure the Babes' one adamant demand from the label: "We just made sure that he put in the contract that we have 100% creative power, so they couldn't tell us how to dress, how to write our songs. What you see is what you get. What you hear is what you get. They signed us, but they won't mold us."[12]

They weren't due in the studio for another six months as 1991 was booked up with touring and promotion for their second and last record with Twin/Tone, *To Mother*. They would tour the UK for two months during the summer (reuniting with Sonic Youth for the famous 1991 Reading Festival captured in *1991: The Year Punk Broke*), record two amazing Peel Sessions, and return to Minneapolis in time to record demos for *Fontanelle* in November before returning abroad for another six-week tour.

In addition to this, they didn't really have a lot of new songs for another full-length album yet. Fifteen songs were needed, and three of them would come from their early years of jamming and experimentation: "Jungle Train," "Short Song," and "Quiet Room," the latter of which had already appeared on *Spanking Machine*. Among the newer songs, "Handsome & Gretel" and "Pearl" were some of the first written and were released as the previously discussed single in 1991.

The other songs were written on the road. By tracing their emergence through available live shows online, it appears the earliest were written around May 1991 where they played "Blood," and "Mother."[13] "Bruise Violet," "Magick Flute," and "Gone" were all ready by late Fall for the Minneapolis demos recorded by Brian Paulson and Lee Ranaldo. By December, the band now had seven songs that they performed regularly, leaving five more that would have to be written in the studio.

"Single-minded in their trio-ness"

The November 1991 demo that the Babes recorded in Minneapolis was certainly more raw and bombastic than the final *Fontanelle*. And a lot of that difference is due to Leon's bass playing. Leon had come into her own by 1991, and was becoming known as an innovative and original bass player impressing musicians such as Lee Ranaldo: "Michelle is just an incredible bass player. She's not an incredible *girl* bass player, she's an incredible bass player. And she's just an amazing, fluid, natural instrumentalist who was all over the bass and doing stuff that supported everything." Even though she was becoming a legend on the stage, it was only now that she felt like she was truly in control of her instrument: "For the first time, I am confident about my bass playing. I don't just hit the same notes as Kat, I create skillful melodies."[14]

This confidence certainly shows in the demos. While usually it's the drums that provide the heartbeat to a band, it is obvious in these tracks that Leon's bass-lines are what's keeping everyone pumping. When they wrote new songs, Barbero would build her rhythm from Leon's lead, and together they provided the rhythmic foundation that allowed Bjelland to riff and caterwaul on the guitar. As such, this perfected dynamic lent a more spontaneous energy to the demo songs. In "Bruise Violet," Bjelland taunts "Liar" playfully, and her singing has become more guttural and boastful. In "Magick Flute" it's hard to distinguish Barbero's contralto from Leon's thunderous baseline. It is played immensely slow, while "Bruise Violet" is faster and more furious.[15]

Ranaldo and Paulson were immensely happy with the demos and were excited about harnessing this raw, live energy within a big studio: "I just remember thinking 'Wow!

This is unbelievable!' They are so rehearsed, and so tight, and so single-minded in their trio-ness." Ranaldo recalled. "They were really tuned in to each other. And it was like locked and loaded and ready to go. Those recordings . . . had all of the energy and purpose and beauty of what those guys were doing at that point as far as I'm concerned."[16]

These new songs also presented an evolving sophistication in Bjelland's lyrics and songwriting, and the band's overall musical compositions: "These were such an exquisite group of songs," Ranaldo recalled. "She [Bjelland] was in such an incredible place in terms of the way she was writing the music and the lyrics." After the demo, they were back on tour in Europe, their *To Mother* set list now being phased out with the new material so they could practice and stay tight for the studio in early 1992. By all accounts, they were perfectly attuned and the path was clearly moving toward a trajectory that only went up. And then things fell out from under them before they could reach the top: "It was remarkable," Ranaldo continued to recall. "And it's kind of tragic that Michelle's not on this record."[17]

Exit Michelle

On October 27, 1990, Michelle Leon had fallen in love with Hole roadie Joe Cole.[18] At the height of their relationship, he was taken from her when he was shot dead on December 19, 1991, during a mugging outside of his Oakland district home. The men got away, and the crime remains unsolved with zero closure to this day.

The Babes were wrapping up the second leg of their six-week European tour. They had one show left when John Peel delivered the news to Leon and the band.[19] She was gutted, and understandably needed space to mourn, but the demands of the band's schedule held no room for it. When she returned to Minneapolis from Cole's funeral, she found it hard to stay interested in practicing and touring, both of which commenced immediately.[20]

Bjelland and Barbero neither could understand Leon's need for solitude nor her growing indifference to recording *Fontanelle*. Leon tried to play through the pain, as her bandmates advised, but found each show more and more draining than therapeutic.

They were scheduled to enter the studio in February, but Ranaldo postponed it until April to finish Sonic Youth's *Dirty*. This postponement did not mean a pause for Leon and the band; it just meant even more touring through the Spring.[21]

Seeing a longer haul of back-to-back tour dates, crammed vans, and cheap hotels, she tried to make things work by requesting for two rooms to be booked rather than one room which always held not only the three women, but their sound men and crew. Leon had hoped by at least just having the band in one room, things would be less rowdy and she could decompress after shows.[22] This doesn't seem like a lot to ask, but Barbero and Bjelland didn't want the band's expenses to increase. Leon's request was denied and she no longer could deny herself. If she couldn't be given the time, or even the space, to come to terms with her life, then she'd have to take matters into her own hands. So, she quit.

Cracks in the Mortar

The story arc of rock bands of the 1990s are all pretty much the same. They come together out of unique and raw talent and youthful verve to create something innovative. They also get good, so good that if they didn't already want to be courted by the major labels, the major labels come a courtin' anyway. The trajectory is always upward until it eventually outpaces the more slower incline of reality—but eventually, reality catches up, and just as it seems like lightning is striking, the band finds it wasn't striking gold or anything as equally transmutable into success, but rather striking in every area that was vulnerable. Cracks in the mortar begin to crawl down the beautiful tower the band had so stellarly ascended, and soon—be it from professional pressures or personal ones (usually a combination of both that are always in opposition to each other) —someone in the band gets thrown out on their ass, taking the rest of the band down with them. Sometimes the metaphorical plummet is quite literal—see Kurt Cobain—or it goes into free fall and the descent lasts for years as it did with the Babes. While their career wasn't instantly incinerated within the flash of the lightning strike, they would never really be able to regain the same momentum they had built with Leon.

Her departure indicated an end to an era as far as what Babes in Toyland meant as a band *at that time*.

Despite all of her contributions and sacrifices, Leon ceases to be part of the story other than what traces of her linger in the revised bass-lines in *Fontanelle*. Although the three women had vowed that if one person left, the Babes would disband, Barbero and Bjelland chose to continue without her. The stakes had changed drastically since their basement days in 1987, and Leon knew that:

> "When you are madly in love and everything is going right, you make all kinds of promises! I 100% expected them to go on without me, expected them to evolve, grow and change. That is not to say it was easy to witness from the sidelines."[23]

Leon's decision was healthy, and the first steps to rebuilding herself from the rubble of her personal Tower, but in doing what she needed, the foundation of the band's structure fell out from under them, and for a while they struggled to keep their momentum.

The system within the band, Babes in Toyland, was very different from the external system the band had to navigate in order to have its major-label career. They were trying to continue to adhere to their artistic ideals, but the original matrilineal spirit conjured by the original formation of Bjelland, Barbero, and Leon would fade into something more *professional*. The band had become their job, so that the external world of the record label saw Leon's leaving as a sudden vacancy needing replacement. When the Babes did fulfill that requirement—they couldn't make an album otherwise—they did about the opposite of what anyone would expect in a situation involving your major-label debut.

They didn't pick someone based on skill or reputation as a session bassist, but selected another old and dear friend who was self-taught and inexperienced, but who would ultimately bring fresh wit and riffs to the Babes, who in exchange would help her come into her own as a musician, just as Leon had.

Enter Maux

"The genesis of me being asked to be in the band," according to Herman. "Was based on large part by the friendship I had with Lori and Kat that went back a long time." While most bands in their situation would have hired a session bassist, they hired someone they knew and trusted, and whose untapped potential to become a great bassist had yet to be realized.

Maureen Herman was born July 25, 1966, making her closer in age to the other two women, but still the youngest member of the band. She was Philadelphia-born but raised in Libertyville, IL. Her family moved to Prior Lake, Minnesota, her senior year, and she relocated to Minneapolis after enrolling at the University.[24]

A long-time punk lover, she quickly got involved in the Heyday and befriended many key figures, including the Cows's Shannon Selberg, who is credited with introducing Herman to Barbero and Bjelland, pre-Babes. Like Barbero, she hadn't been called to really play until her twenties despite her long-time immersion within music. But Fate called when her bass-playing brother mauled his hand in a work accident and gave her his instrument.[25]

Around the same time, she had just witnessed the first Babes basement show Leon had, and became inspired to start a band of her own: "And I had also started playing in bands and I had a practice space in the basement and they [Bjelland and Barbero] didn't know that I even played really because I had just started . . . they kind of did because Kat taught me how to tune a guitar . . . but you know, I wasn't like a big player."[26]

About a year after that, around 1989, Herman relocated to Chicago and became close friends with Steve Albini, roomed with members of The Jesus Lizard, and fell in love with the scene that revolved around indie label Touch and Go Records. Despite her punk rock relationships, she was on a steady and stable academic path. She enrolled in graduate school for English at Columbia College Chicago, and earned tuition working in the English Department. To stay in practice with the bass, she played with the bar-band Cherry Rodriguez in the evenings. She was set on a path to become a writer, but then in 1992, during Valentine's Day weekend, Babes in Toyland were in Chicago with Dinosaur, Jr. and My Bloody Valentine. The Babes always crashed on Herman's floor, but this time only Barbero and Bjelland stayed over:

> At that time, Michelle was wanting to slow down the touring . . . . And the success of the rock and roll business came first. I always thought that was a big mistake—she put in a lot of time, . . . and she didn't get to hit the jackpot, and to me, I don't know, I would have waited and told the record label to hold on a second we got something going on, but that's not how it went down.

A month later, Herman got a phone call from Barbero asking her to audition.[27] Her roommate Duane Denison, of The

Jesus Lizards, taught her all of the Babes songs before she went to Minneapolis for the audition. As a result: "I fucking nailed it." She was in, starting immediately.

Herman was hesitant at first. She would have to immediately enter the nomadic and economically unstable life of a working rock band. Despite regularly jamming in Cherry Rodriguez, Herman was just starting to get familiar with her instrument. Even though she nailed the parts on the Babes' previous albums, she'd have to learn all of the new ones for *Fontanelle*, all while touring, before zooming in to the studio. In addition to facing this hairpin-learning curve, she would have to drop out of her program, quit her job, and put her literary aspirations on hold:

> And then it was like getting up to speed—had to take pictures—and it was a difficult decision for me because I was in a place in my life where I worked hard to get to. I was in school studying writing, and I had a full-time job with benefits that paid for the school and it was a good stable time for me and I was going to throw it all away to tour.[28]

But after confiding her doubts to a friend, she realized this was a once-in-a-lifetime opportunity: "I talked to different people, like Steve Albini, and they said you'll never get another chance to see the world the way you will in a band, and these other opportunities will be there when you get back."[29]

This was a huge leap of faith, considering Herman would not be cut in financially for her time on the record. She wasn't experienced enough in the industry to ask to be written into the royalties, and it appears at no point during the recording of *Fontanelle* did anyone think to suggest she should, even when Herman donated the riffs for "Right Now," a song she wrote while in Cherry Rodriguez. In what will be discussed more later, Herman also rewrote many of Leon's previous bass-lines to better fit her own style of playing.

> I think it was fair she [Leon] got the advance as kind of a payback for all the work she did. But when it came to writing the album, I was writing my bass parts and in some cases, like "Right Now" I was writing the song. . . . They didn't write it, I did. But I didn't feel that way about it because I wasn't aware of all of that stuff and how it plays our financially. I did later, and it mattered. . . . I always felt like it was a little unfair that I didn't get any royalties for *Fontanelle*.

Herman would receive royalties for her participation in the live CBGB recording on *Painkillers*, but not for the Side A tracks: "It wasn't until *Nemesisisters* that things were set up the way they should be. And I was too naive at the time to understand all of that."[30]

Herman was all in, and was immediately on the road with the Babes, sometime around March 17, 1992. They would tour for two weeks and then settle in New York City the week of March 30, to start their first round of recording at Sorcerer's Studio.

"I had a lot to fucking learn," Herman reflected. "Not just the songs, but how touring was, and who the different players were in terms of management . . . . But I felt like I was being welcomed in as a full member in as much as you could in that short span of time."

Herman had to pick up the new songs immediately, and while on stage: "I had the notes for the songs written in my own weird music language in a sharpie on the floor of the stage. I had no idea what I was fucking doing, so it was all very quick. It took me a while to get comfortable on stage."[31]

Uncomfortable or not, by the CBGB performance the night before they went into Sorcerer's Studio, Herman wasn't missing a beat. But just as she was starting to hold her own on stage, she found that the recording studio would become a whole other beast to slay.

Plate 4
The Quiet Room

Recording *Fontanelle* would prove much more challenging than the Babes' earlier albums. While the Babes had knocked every previous album out within four to five days, *Fontanelle* would be drawn out over a four-week schedule: four days at Sorcerer's Studio in Brooklyn, and three weeks at Pachyderm Studios in Cannon Falls, Minnesota. Barbero and Bjelland had begun rebuilding the band with Herman, but their foundation remained shaky while they all got to know each other in the studio. As a result, it would fall on Herman, Ranaldo, and Paulson to stabilize this new version of the band. While at first it seemed to the Babes that recording for a month was an excessive amount of time, it would turn out they needed every minute they could get.

The four days in New York City were more for Reprise's benefit than the band. According to Karlen, this was a tactic to "keep an eye" on the band during the first days and make sure everything started off on a solid foundation. It was also an opportunity to work on the marketing and promotional side of things, including a photo shoot with Michael Lavine, meet and greet with Warner Brother bigwigs and their new manager, Debbie Gordon. Barbero and Herman visited Cindy Sherman's studio to pick out the cover image, and preview the album with a CBGB showcase, an invite-only performance for music critics and art influencers who could promote Babes in Toyland in more mainstream and artistic avenues.[1] It was a great performance and its recording would appear as a B-side on *Painkillers* in 1993.

Not only did the Babes need to write a few more songs, but Herman's intuitive playing style meant she had to rework many of Leon's lines:

> I never listened to the demo because I didn't want to play what Michelle played. We were different players. She played with her fingers, and I played with a pick, and I just wanted to do my own thing. And then I have a hard time covering other songs. I play by ear, so it was easier for me to have them play and I'd come up with the bass part, and that's pretty much how we did all the songs.[2]

It sounds perfectly natural, but in an expensive and professional studio, in front of producers and engineers, it was less than ideal:

> That was tough . . . . Like: "Oh, Lee from Sonic Youth? Hi! I don't know how to fucking play like a normal person." I play by ear, I didn't go to school for it, I didn't know what to fucking do, so the way I learned was by playing with people better than me. . . . and it felt weird, because of course I'm going to hit wrong notes because I don't know what I'm playing yet. And he's like "Just play in G" and I'm

like "I don't know what that means." Everything was by ear, so that was just . . . I felt lost and judged and pressured to see my weird creative musical process exposed to others when it otherwise wouldn't have been—I was self conscious about it.

If Herman thought Ranaldo seemed frustrated, it was because no one had informed him of the change of bassist until the very last minute. He assumed that he and Brian Paulson would pick up where they had left off in November 1991. When Ranaldo discovered that Leon was gone, and that her replacement was still getting up to speed on her bass-lines: "It was just like [being in] a car that's going 80 miles an hour (with Michelle) come screeching to a halt and starts creeping along at like 2 miles an hour."

The original plan had been to lay down the bass and drum tracks during the four days at Sorcerer's. That seemed to be accomplished to everyone's satisfaction, but when they got to Pachyderm and played the tracks back, Ranaldo found them wanting. He and Paulson would have to rethink their strategies to assist Herman with her parts, get her some better gear, and help the band regain the synchronicity that they had exhibited in Minneapolis.

Ranaldo's goal was to recreate the band live. Like on the demo, the band would record in the same room and do a few takes of each song, and from each song the best of each instrument would be patched together to create an uber-sound. Vocals would be enhanced with overdubbing, and only then certain notes or phrases would be re-recorded and tweaked to ensure everything lined up. In order to do this, you had to have a solid drum track, and according to Ranaldo, Barbero was being thrown off by the new dynamic in the band: "With the demos, the three of them set up in the room and just had at it, and maybe we overdubbed new vocals or something like that, but it was just all there and they were playing live together. And they couldn't do that with Maureen."

Of course, the new synchronicity would come with time, but in an expensive studio with a tight schedule, time was not on their side. To try to resolve this, they scrapped their plan of recording live, and began to focus on each instrument separately. But while the band still wasn't tight when they played together, playing separately threw them off even more. According to Herman:

> It didn't work. We started it that way but we ended up doing it the other way, a lot of it, because it wasn't fucking working. I needed to see Lori and be by Lori, and just the energy—it was flat. Me standing in a fucking isolation booth, or whatever, playing bass by myself while everyone is staring at me is probably not going to get the best performance, ya know.

Paulson and Ranaldo brainstormed several methods, including the use of a click track to try and get everything to sync: "I mean things had changed so much in those few short weeks," Paulson reflected. "That it got to the point that we were basically trying anything we could to find something that was remotely close." They focused on nailing down the drum tracks first, then the bass tracks, and this process took most of the three weeks.

Ranaldo was under a lot of pressure from Carr and the studio to make a *Nevermind*-style hit on schedule. Paulson, who had been friends with Herman pre-Babes, was able to help her through the trickier parts of finishing her tracks. In fact, these moments would become Paulson's favorite memories of the experience: "I oddly enjoyed really trying to help Maureen become comfortable in this new scenario. I remember we sort of kicked everyone out and were like 'it's time to do your bass.' I've always really tried to create a safe space as possible so they [musicians] can do the best they can." Herman and Paulson would sit in the studio together troubleshooting notes and the isolated parts that needed re-recording here and there.

Personally, I admire Maureen for going for it. This has been an overarching theme of the band that really contributed to how fast-tracked they seemed. From the barbecue in 1986 on, members of Babes in Toyland never dawdled over an opportunity. The only exception might be signing with Warner Brothers, and oddly enough I think that had some consequences for them. But they never waited for perfection or sat around while the stars took their time to align . . . they grabbed their gear and got on the road and practiced while performing. They didn't care about attaining perfection, only momentum, and they swooped Herman up in this same manner and spirit. She was obviously a perfect match because she was courageous enough to go for it. It was tough as hell on her, but she persevered, wrote her bass-lines, and ended up bringing a new warmth to the band's future songs.

Time is finite. If you are going to do something, do it now. Finish it when you need to finish it, while the going is hot.

You can always fix it later, or if you can't, you learn from it. The Babes were being creative in a time when perfection or expertise wasn't expected of its artists. They were allowed to experiment in public, be messy, and not be held accountable for what didn't work. If they had been, they never would have progressed beyond their first show. Herman may not have been prepared for *Fontanelle* and the major-label studio experience, but she worked through it, and became an amazing musician for it.

Throughout this rigorous process, the Babes wrote or rewrote five songs that hadn't been on previous set lists. Herman added an entirely new bass-line to "Jungle Train" and the band collaborated on "Right Now," "Won't Tell," and "Spun":

> A lot of the times, it was the verse part I would do, and Kat would have the chorus parts, but it was just collaborative. They would just play the songs repeatedly while I fucked around until I found a groove. And they [Kat and Lori] never told me, "No, Michelle does it like this; or No It goes like this." They just played it over and over again until I came up with my part.

At the time, Herman didn't realize that she was revamping the band's very first song:

> So basically, I forgot about that, and I didn't know about that at the time, but you know to me it was just another song that I had to come up with my part for. It just felt like a jam, the way they explained it to me, they called it the

meth song, everyone is just going fucking nuts. But I felt like I added a lot to that with the way I played it.

Herman's favorite memory of this time involved recording "Quiet Room":

> You know, there was a lot of, like, people around, and Kat and I hadn't really had much alone time, just in general. Everybody wanted her ear, whether it was the engineer, Lori, Tim Carr, or Lee, and we had this connection when we would play that was wordless. I can't explain it, but she would fill in the cracks, and I would fill in the cracks and crevices, and we'd meet—and it was this thing that we would do.

> And we sat on the floor of the studio, and she played "Quiet Room," and it was the only time she pointed out the notes to me—like where to start, here's the key—and, she played it and we did it in one take. It was just this really kind of private, us sitting there, me and Kat playing together, and it was just so cool because I remember her teaching me how to tune my guitar back when I was just starting to figure music out and here we were.

At the beginning of the track you can hear Bjelland call out to Herman: "She goes 'Maux!' I go 'What?' and we start playing . . . I always loved that that was on the actual record."

While there are moments in *Fontanelle* when it is hard to hear Herman's bass, on "Quiet Room" it rings clear, and it adds a beautiful warm comfort to the song. Perhaps it was due to the camaraderie captured on tape, but this recording seems more organic and alive than the *Spanking Machine* version. This may have been due to it being one of the rare tracks where Herman was comfortable: "I made up the part, but she showed me where to start. I loved it, I loved how it came out. It was just a really special moment that we had and that kind of camaraderie that Kat and I shared was something that was heralded later when we would reunite. It was that same kind of thing."

Through trial and error, Ranaldo and Paulson eventually got the tracks they needed from Barbero and Herman, and all that was left were to get Bjelland's guitars and vocals done.

"Kat just blazed through it." Paulson remembered.

It was effortless for her. Guitars, done. Vocals, done. No question, no second guessing, no nothing; it was just like—that's it. Her energy definitely carries a lot of that. And that was probably the missing element. Everything was being picked apart. It's easy to put everything under a microscope, which you should not do with a group like that, but it happened.

While Bjelland's sessions were no sweat, the mixing would become contentious. There was a lot of pressure on the band—as there now was on every band after September 1991—to be the new Nirvana. Suddenly studios expected their noisome, rough, risky bets to be platinum blockbusters. Pressure was on Ranaldo to be the next Butch Vig, but the joke was that no one, not even Vig, had anticipated *Nevermind's* success, and no one could reproduce that result. As Paulson joked: "The Nirvana thing. It was such an anomaly. It's not like the record companies even made that happen. It was the timing, it was the people that decided . . . . So, you are being told to create that magic again, that's not definable whatsoever!"

While the Babes had been signed to Warner Brothers before Nirvana became a household name, the possibilities hung in the air, and Ranaldo knew that "Tim, Warner Brothers, was really anxious that it be a really good record."

As the expectations mounted, Bjelland's anxiety rose as the record went into overtime and over budget. She began to second guess the direction Ranaldo and Paulson were taking the album. By the end of the month, Bjelland had become displeased with the mixes, and Ranaldo was fired.[3] Brian Paulson had been asked to finish it, first, but Paulson turned it down, already burnt out from working eighteen hours a day on it with no breaks:

> To be honest, it makes sense that those mixes got nixed, because I was fried at that point. I remember when that process got unplugged, Tim Carr reaching out to me immediately and saying "Look, they want you to finish the record without Lee." And I was like, "I need at least a week" and Tim was like "We can't wait that long." And I was like "I'm sorry I can't, I'm not going to be able to jump back into it tomorrow and do a good job." I was fried. I'd barely slept in like a month and a half.

While Paulson was out, he would be on hand to handle questions from Skinny Puppy's Dave Ogilve, who worked with Bjelland through a solid week of fourteen hour days in Chicago. This work, alongside her ideas of ambient noise and layering of vocals earned Bjelland co-producer credit with Lee Ranaldo.[4]

Although Bjelland never really explained to him why she disliked the mix, Ranaldo empathizes with the move:

> This was their first major label record, and it was a major label making a first record with a new kind of band out of this kind of unknown indie scene . . . . Kat was hearing the mixes come back, and it was a completely different sound spectrum than she'd ever heard her band make before . . . . There were overdubs and vocal overdubs and all that kind of stuff, but I just have to say that Sonic Youth went through the exact same thing as this when we made our first record for Geffen.

Ranaldo believes Bjelland got a case of cold feet, as Sonic Youth had when making their major-label debut, *Goo*. They were initially working with Nick Sansano, who produced *Daydream Nation*, but the pressure of major-label expectations got the best of the band:

> We started mixing with him, and between band and label, knowing this is your major label debut we were all like "Gee, I wonder if it's good enough?" And it was almost as though no matter what it sounded like it wasn't going to satisfy your expectations of what it should be as the major label debut.

Just as Carr had done to Ranaldo, Sonic Youth "pulled the plug on Nick Sansano and hired some hot shot mixing guy to mix *Goo*. It's the exact same story." At the end of the day,

Ranaldo believes there was nothing innately wrong with where the mixes were going, rather that Bjelland was looking for something else:

> Dave Ogilve is a studio guy; Brian and I were an indie rock scene, and we wanted them to have a vérite quality and all that stuff, and the major labels didn't know what they wanted these records to be. And I remember [talking to] Tim . . . about it afterwards and him saying 'we just didn't know if we were getting everything we could have out of those mixes, and wanted to try something different.' And I suppose Kat felt the same way, and she was the only one who really had a vote on what it'd sound like, basically.

Fontanelle was now late, and more than $30,000 over budget, but at least it was ready to be mastered by Howie Weinberg at Masterdisk in New York and delivered to Reprise.[5]

By June, and with two months before release, *Fontanelle* was completed.

The End Result

No matter the mix, Babes in Toyland were never going to be radio-friendly. As Paulson confided: "That was one of the things that contributed to all of the anxieties. There is no magic formula we can apply to this that is going to guarantee you success on the air waves." But for a noise band like Babes in Toyland, *Fontanelle* did get pretty close. The album does have that Butch Vig clarity, where everything is crystal clear without losing the Babes' swampy layers of distortion. When you compare this version of "Quiet Room" to the *Spanking Machine* version, there is no fuzzy distortion. The guitar almost rings with the clarity of a harpsichord.

What is most striking about *Fontanelle* is Bjelland's vocals. Her voice is intelligible and more prominent over the instrumentals than in any previous recordings. The layering of overdubs creates a chorus of Kat's answering and responding to the queries of her catharsis, giving it an Ancient Greek sense of hubris and crisis. In the case of "Jungle Train," which now featured lyrics in addition to Herman's new bass-line, Bjelland creates a haunting soundscape with only two violent words repeated and rolled around in her diaphragm as various shrieks, wails, frays, and shouts. They all boil and bubble over each other to create a sense of overhearing eldrich incantations in some primal, forbidden grove.

Carr arranged the tracks, and followed an auditory rather than a thematic progression. He felt there was a monotony-risk, that the songs could bleed into each other as one continuous track—so he tried to break the tempos and hooks up and create variety.[6] I don't know what the original tracking order was, but the way Carr arranged it does make it feel theatrical, especially with the epilogue of "Gone," where Bjelland uses environmental sound to create an eerie and intimate blues song with crushing bottles and ear-splitting wails. It was as evocative to record, as Ranaldo reminisced: "That song had this kind of dark, late night, moody vibe, and . . . I remember her tapping with a bottle and making a rhythmic thing, and we were like why don't you go in and record that, and it ended up with her smashing the bottles and that sounded even better, and so we did some more of that."

While these effects and emphasis on voice give listeners a sample of Bjelland's vocal range and repertoire, *Fontanelle* adds lucidity to one of Bjelland's most overlooked and under discussed accomplishments—her lyrics.

Posterior Fontanelle

Kat Bjelland's lyrics do what all great art should do—open a portal into another's inner world. *Fontanelle* is about female friendship, doppelgängers, emotionally and physically abusive relationships, mental health, and drug abuse. Her treatments of these difficult topics aren't triggering, however, but rather empowering, as Liz Evans observed in *Women, Sex, and Rock 'n' Roll*: "In blowing up the boundaries of acceptable female emotion," Evans writes, "Bjelland Grey [*sic*] reminds people that if women are to be understood and appreciated as human beings, they must be given the rights to express everything they feel, whether good or really, really bad."[1]

Bjelland rewards close reading—something she very rarely receives. Overall, her lyrics feature a stark confessional realism crossed with surrealistic fantasies that mix fairy tale logic with nursery rhyme cant. Each song is an autobiographical collage of experiences and relationships, her dreams and nightmares, all infused with an intimate and personal magical symbolism. The thoughts are immensely fragmented and internal, and we'll never have the right keys to pick the locks to her personal mythos. But, as listeners, we can try.

Bjelland's shard-like lyrics penetrate the brain with lovely hooks and disarming refrains that become lodged in the hearer's head that then transmits her words into our own personal transmutations. Interpreting them is a lot like scrying—there are multiple ripples and layers one can contemplate, and whether it's a surface or deep-dive reading, the interpretations transmute themselves into the listeners' heart and become personally identifiable, like a mantra.

The characters in Bjelland's lyrics are often referred to as "girls," but she only wrote songs about young women learning to navigate the joys and sorrows of their existence—all broken mirrored reflections of herself. These vignettes are confessional and conversational fragments sewn together to make an experiential collage depicting violence committed against themselves or vengeance against others. They are songs about women losing and regaining power. Men are present, but their presence is secondary, background, off-screen even. And while that is all serious stuff, there's still room for whimsy.

Magic, and from it a kind of tortured divinity, permeates Bjelland's lyrics—composing the most obscure aspects of her personal lyrical language, this magic is only revealed at close scrutiny, and often contains entire spells and systems within one or two words. In "22" on *Nemesisters*, Bjelland invents an entire new vocabulary built upon transforming the names of various obscure and forgotten Goddesses into verbs, adjectives, and active nouns, including Agasaya a Sumarian warrior goddess known for her powerful shrieking. These magical interests can be found within a few words here and there, sprinkled throughout *Spanking Machine* and *To Mother,* but becomes more developed within *Fontanelle.*

In the Evans interview, Bjelland acknowledges the role magical thinking plays in her lyrics through nightmares and even the divine feminine: "I'm really obsessed with babies and angels too and I'm sure it's to do with my dreams . . . . Maybe it's to do with the whole birth thing, with a woman being like a universe in herself. Well, that's how I think of the universe, like someone's huge womb."[2]

From scar-sucking confessionalism to magical mythos, Bjelland's use of perspective change blends experience together into sort of a Futurist flurry where the past, present, and future all expand and collide on the same plane through simple changes in pronouns and wordplay transmutations: "My songs are really personal but a lot of the time I shroud the meanings on purpose. I write in metaphors and symbolism and double meanings and get them all tangled up, so you have to be at least into it or clever enough to untangle it."[3] She goes on to describe her process as therapeutic, and only writes when troubled, never when content or having fun. As a result, she considers sad music like Leonard Cohen, Nick Cave, and Billie Holiday are more relatable to her as art.

Paging Sylvia Plath

Bjelland was also impressed and inspired by the poetry of Sylvia Plath, especially the *Ariel* poems, Plath's most famous and inventive collection that includes "Lady Lazarus" and "Daddy." Bjelland has referenced Plath in a few songs throughout her career—she borrows the line "We both drag our Jesus hair around" in "Dust Cake Boy" from Plath's

"Medusa" ("Dragging their Jesus hair")[4] and names a song on *Nemesisters* "Ariel."

The titular poem provides an excellent example of Plath's appeal. On the surface, it is about a horse ride at dawn; the horse is inspired by Plath's childhood pet of the same name. But when you go beyond the keyhole to pick the poem's lock, it begins to take on mythological, personal, feminist, and creative significance—all filtered through Plath's personal experience. Bjelland utilizes the same sort of layering in her lyrics where sometimes one word carries the entire poem (it's amazing how much mileage she gets out of a few words when they are performed) and, in doing so, transforms its meaning.

Plath refused to perpetuate the same male notions of women's poetry and set out to create her own mythology mixing domestic discomforts with psychoanalysis and a wide range of religious and classic mythology. Through those filters she wrote about mental health, depression, and alienation in an honest and visceral way no poet had ever done before. She revealed the darkness of her experience and its womanhood, and it was either seen as genius or off-putting to her peers. She earned the reputation of being a sad and angry woman.

Plath was intent on giving the ugliness in her experience a beautiful form, and I think what Plath most taught Bjelland was that the mundanities of one's life held the potential for alchemy. Through art, music, and her lyrics, Bjelland was able to navigate her experiences with the various forms of abuse (be it drug, physical, sexual, or emotional) and through her own personal interpretations of language and symbolism transmute herself into a place of power. But Bjelland takes Plath's anger a step further.

As dissonant and jarring as Plath's poetry can be, her domain is constricted by academia and domesticity. She's angry and passionate, but she's not loud. Her words are measured hexes spoken under one's breath, just out of ear shot of the fathers and husbands that might retort or retaliate. It's a trapped appeal—her poems show you the stitches, and you know the threads are holding together deep and volcanic wounds. She has been hurt and hounded and haunted. She stands in a soft focus of power in which she knows she's independent but not free. Harsh words will spit through clinched teeth, but she'll never raise her voice and say "fuck you."

Bjelland doesn't have this problem. People are being told off and where to go throughout all of Bjelland's lyrics. Whereas Plath utilized the confession of "I," Bjelland wields the confrontation of "you."

Despite how deeply personal and autobiographical the songs are, even the most obscure semiotics are relatable and memorable. Her images are visceral and searing—and through each song is a signal darting through the screams, distortion, and toms to punch you right in the gut. Below are the signals I have been picking up for over thirty years. The signal is different to each and every listener, and so you may interpret something else. That is the power of Bjelland's lyrics—not only did she use the form to regain power for herself, but despite how personal the words are, they are still relatable enough for others to find their own meaning and empowerment.

Handsome and Gretel

In "Handsome and Gretel," Bjelland suggests the premise and ideas associated with the famous Grimm fairy tale. Beyond the title's allusion, all similarities cease. The characters aren't lost in a forest full of sweet temptations, but a hellscape full of sexual exploitation in which the archetypical Gretel is forced to prostrate herself before countless apathetic lovers.

The perspective see-saws between the two eponymous characters, their destitute confusion melding together into a debauch dialogue of almost "he said/she said" but delves deeper into the psychological damage being done. The song isn't sticky with gingerbread houses and icicle icing, but with dried semen, smack, and swear-spit that can never be taken back.

Gretel calls other women cunts and fucking bitches, and these slurs are often slung throughout *Fontanelle*. This caused a lot of controversy for the band as they entered the mainstream. Because the swears weren't used in a sexual sense, the band was able to evade an Explicit Lyrics warning label,[5] but they couldn't escape finger-wags from the press, and Bjelland was often chided for her semantics: "A male journalist once criticized me for calling women cunts in one of my songs. But if anyone can say it, I can! I have one! I can say whatever I want, . . . I don't always want to be saying the right thing."[6]

The helpless filth of the song gets quickly flipped as it changes key to wind down. It becomes suddenly terse, clipped, and abstract. One word, "Asphixia," anchors and transitions this section from hear-tell about Handsome and Gretel, but into Gretel's head where we see flashes of the sexual assault she's been subjected to. This becomes a moment of powerful recovery for Gretel. Where she is pinned down and throttled to the point of unconsciousness, the "Asphixia," the power dynamic, is flipped. Her forced-open thighs now become weaponized as vices. And even though we are shown these scenes through Imagistic brevity, the power is reverted in a common dialogue of denial so painfully familiar in abusive relationships—Gretel vehemently still loves Handsome. It's co-dependency at its most horrific, a domestic scene that goes way over any of the amphetamine edges Sylvia Plath dare walk.

Bluebell

"Bluebell" is an excellent example of Bjelland's confessional mythos collage style. It opens with a bit of fantasy and word play turned sinister, and references the nineteenth-century song popularized by vaudeville in the 1920s, "The Daring Young Man on the Flying Trapeze." She upcycles the song's first two lines to make it seem like Bluebell is physically flying, but when we are told she "takes little pills and calls them trapeze," flying is just her very grounded state of being fucked up.

Bjelland toys with the sing-song innocence of this classic circus song and turns the effortless expectations projected onto femininity into what it is, a disease. It's an image of being set free from consciousness and societal mores, only to be shot back down to the ground by the off-screen conversational accusations of someone who thinks they know better.

It would be tempting to try to tie Bluebell's descent to the myth of Persephone, especially when the song's most famous line warning against raping goddesses is shrieked. It could be a very interesting response to the complicity the Gods had when Demeter appealed to them about her daughter's abduction to Hades. But as the last line accuses, that might be too obvious. Why this line isn't a #metoo slogan, I just don't know. It perfectly captures the duality of Feminism's empowerment and vulnerability in one breath. With Gorganic petrification, it calls out the perpetrator and punishes him with woman's full collective fury.

Blood

Beyond the personal/confessional, Bjelland's lyrics are hard to crack beyond the surface, but if you dig deep down, you find glittering geodes. "Blood" shows Bjelland at the height of her sphinx-like sophistication as a songwriter. It describes someone who can't get away from herself even in the company of others, and feels forced to suppress her emotions through other's humors. In this instance, it is blood, where she very cleverly juxtaposes this sanguine nature with her own melancholia.

The Four Humors appear throughout many of her songs, including *Spanking Machine* and *To Mother*, but here it is so subtle it's easy to miss. Developed by Hippocrates in ancient Greece, the humors composed the embryonic systems of psychology. It was an attempt to try and understand our mind-body connection and the effect emotions had on our overall health and constitution. It also would become intertwined within alchemical and other metaphysical systems, as each humor not only corresponded with body fluids, but with the seasons, elements, astrology, food, and even stages of life like adolescence and old age.[7] This system dominated medical practice well up until the eighteenth century. Even today, you can see its roots in every personality exam as complex as Meyers-Brigg or simple as the True Colors Test.

The name of the song points to a sanguine nature—those with too much blood. They were extroverted and enjoyed being part of the crowd. They dreaded boredom and as a result engaged in a lot of risk taking behaviors. In modern psychology, a sanguine nature would be akin to a manic phase of a personality disorder.

The song's title alludes to a sanguine but disingenuous disposition. It's actually a deep, dark, internal secret of the melancholiac, and perhaps even a paean to the creative process that has been associated with melancholia since Aristotle, and especially overshadows that of female poets like Sylvia Plath. "Blood" is perhaps a little joke about Bjelland's introversion (Bjelland would be diagnosed with Schizoaffective Disorder in 2007), and how the creative process could be kind of like a blood letting—or at the very least—a portal out of the black abyss.

In "Blood," rather than overflowing, the body is violently expelling, exploding, imploding, and fending off boredom (the bane of the melancholic). When she sings about infusion, it almost sounds like she's allowing something else to mix within—a cosmic blood transfusion that would give her a desire for more outward exuberance. And it's all anchored by an evocative and cryptic placation of "Dear Liver."

It seems like word play on "dear lover," but Bjelland could also be toying with the humors, where once upon a time people believed the liver functioned as the heart, producing blood of the outgoing, shiny happy people.[8] While "Dear Liver" seems like an apology to the substances foisted on the overworked processing organ, when you look at it from a humoral perspective, it becomes a plea for more sanguinity, for more extroversion, an attribute society at large awards, even in excess, over introversion. With this bit of arcane trivia, the appeal seems to transpose "lover" with "liver" to mix together the sanguine and melancholic dispositions into one entity at war with itself, so much, that the narrator questions her own integrity and identity by the song's end.

Won't Tell

"Won't Tell" plays with narrative voice in an operatic fashion. It see-saws from sweet and docile to enraged and confrontational, using the language as anchors for each monkey bar swing of emotion. It's easy to equate this as a love song—but this kind of co-dependent confrontation can pertain to any interpersonal relationship where power is at play. I see the repeats between the verse and chorus, the see saw between naught and nice, as the repeat of an abusive cycle—perhaps inspired by Bjelland's childhood. There's the frustration felt from her biological mother abandoning her with an abusive step-mother who inflicted deep psychological wounds rather than nurture and comfort. "I wait forever for you" almost seems like a lament for her real mother to come back, while the verse is a placating plea used to deflect further harm. Both mothers have problems that they never figure out and instead project them onto Bjelland's inner child. Through oscillations in Bjelland's voice, she depicts the wounded child's vulnerability through docile whispers; while the healed child, now adult, is able to channel her own power and confronts those who wounded through bold and clear shouts.

Right Now

"Right Now" deals with child abuse and its ability to freeze you in time through traumatic recall. The narrator remembers being a child while saying her prayers before bed. The rote emphasis of being of service and servitude to others is ironic. It's just the sort of brainwashed purpose that can easily push vulnerable people into harm's path rather than protect them. She's afraid to go to sleep for fear of an unnamed boogy man who's obviously visited her in the night before. It's one of her more fragmentary songs, and it's not entirely clear if she's referencing sexual abuse or just traumatic nightmares. But with the utterance of two violent and alliterative words she's able to make it applicable to anyone who wears a "scarred surface" from their youth.

Underneath this scarred surface, a callous that's grown from infancy through adulthood, there is a deeper inner child wounding. As each verse explores traumatic recall, the chorus shakes the narrator out of it by erupting into its powerful mantra that you have to live in the now. It's an empowering reminder of survival and confronting the past in order to not repeat it, or to keep letting it drag you down.

Mother

Perhaps a maternal counterpart to Plath's "Daddy," this song comes in punching. Unlike the traumatic recollections in "Right Now" and "Won't Tell," there are no childlike vulnerabilities or innocence here. There's a revenge vibe—its tone is vindictive and confrontational, but also a mature acknowledgment of a power dynamic flip between an indifferent mother who gives life and a rivaling sibling who threatens to take it away. The whole tension of the song is between two sisters, one who seems to be more vulnerable and abused than the other, but by the end of the song, the cycle of abuse is acknowledged to have encircled both siblings as "You are obscene" is inverted to conclude with "You are me."

This inversion of "I," "you," or "me" see-saws throughout the entire song. In the first version of the chorus, the narrator sings in the first person, but by the second version "me" is replaced with "you," changing the placement of blame from the narrator on to who is truly afflicting her (be it the mother or the sister).

Through oscillating pronouns, power dynamics are flipped within every progressing verse. What begins as a desire for control over others collapses into confusion and becomes a struggle to control one's self. Another angle of this narrative could be that perhaps there isn't a physical sister at all, but a twinning of self—a doppelgänger—where through disassociation the narrator is witnessing her own abuse and trying to regain her power through it. Between misplaced blame, either on oneself or projected on to those who wouldn't help, or were helpless themselves.

Pearl

Pearl is about an eponymous junky. It plays with a lot of feminized smack slang where names like "Black Pearl," "Black Tar," "Brown Sugar," and "Aunt Hazel" have all referred to heroin at some point in time. In this song, however, the opiate is referred to as "black sugar shit."

Despite its nursery rhyme cant, it doesn't glamorize the drug. It explores Pearl's motivations for shooting up that tie back to the humors where melancholia permeates the entire vibe with inky textures. Pearl is suffering from some kind of unnamed mental illness, which at times seems like immense anxiety compounded by hopelessness and harm to herself and others. She takes succor in the "black sugar shit" to numb and escape herself, and she does that to the point of overdosing and hospitalization.

The imagery in this song is masterful. The tools Pearl uses to cook down heroin also serves as a metaphor for Pearl's overall situation. Like her spoon, she's bent out of shape and insane. But the most visceral image is conjured by "Devilspit," which describes how heroin appears after it's cooked down. The single word conjures white, frothy bubbles boiling in the tar pit of the spoon.

Addiction itself is symbolized by a blackbird, which is always shrieking in her head to find surcease in her sorrows through more drugs. It's a really cool image because not only does it harken back to the poor bird that met its sonic demise in the Babes' practice basement, but also alludes to the Christian symbolism of the blackbird as an avatar of the Devil himself, which neatly refers back to the devilspit-drug and the existential demons that drove Pearl to self-medicate. Having survived this overdose, Pearl wants to go clean, concluding at the end that the heroin hasn't helped her deal with her problems. All it did was lead to more bullshit.

Spun

"Spun" is about trying to keep it together and not let other people get the best of you. It also could easily be attributable to self-perception and the perception of others, especially media. By this time in the Babes' career, the band was becoming famous. With it came notoriety, unwanted attention, and media spin.

When doing promotion for a project, you are forced to open yourself up to complete strangers, and many of them aren't friendlies, especially if they get the sense you hate it. Throughout the chorus, Bjelland sounds so desperate to evade the limelight, that she chokes like a little mouse after a powerful sustain of "out."

It's an interesting take to think of because the celebrity experience has become so mundane by today's standards. With the ubiquity of social media in everyday life, most people are celebrities in their world, but the thing is they have control of their image and their content and for the most part can fly their own kite around.

But in the 1990s, bands were susceptible to the adoration or scorn of the media. You were left dependent upon them to correct anything they got wrong or misconstrued, which they rarely did. Some celebrities learned to grow into theses dynamics and leverage it for more fame, but the Babes had no interest in creating or maintaining any sort of image. And because they wouldn't play the game, they found themselves chewed up and spat out by the media.

Utilizing synesthesia as evocatively as Fitzgerald or Plath, this crowd "is green with rivalry." It's a roiling sea of potential money and fame, but comes with the price of drowning your true self, as the jarring chiasmus concludes.

Realeyes

"Realeyes" is an anti-love song. It's very evocative of how distant someone right next to you can feel, and about the complex emotions experienced after leaving someone. It contains one of Bjelland's most interesting lines which is immensely esoteric and gets three puns for the price of one: (Hear tic-toc/Here tic-toc).

I'm unsure whether Bjelland's upbringing was Catholic, but Catholic themes do permeate her songs. In this instance, she alludes to the manner in which early Catholicism tried to track Easter, which never has a set date within the Gregorian calendar.[9] Here it is used as a deadline; the narrator won't stand another season with this person.

The chorus has an interesting breakdown of puns, word play, and slow realizations. The first "realize" is like a dawning of the truth, further opened up with "real eyes" that continue to oscillate between the two words. By the third utterance of it, the "I's" within the words bounce throughout the rest of the chorus, but this alliteration isn't about rhymes. It harkens back to Plath's definitive "I," where self-truths are being uncovered and proclaimed. The amazing screaming breakdown at the end, layered so it presents all of Bjelland's banshee ranges, becomes a release valve for her frustration with the failed relationship.

Gone

The last and most haunting song on *Fontanelle*, "Gone" is perhaps the most produced song on the album, and to great effect. Bjelland plays solo with no change within its riff structure or rhythm. The only fluctuation is directed by Bjelland's vocals and its various overlays of harmonies and environmental noise. For the chorus, there are multiple layers of Bjelland singing "It's Gone," that gives it a spooky sense of response from the underworld spirits. In the background, the bottles burst and crash punctuations to blood-curdling shrieks and wails. It's the soundtrack to someone's mental breakdown.

Bjelland says that "it was about Kurt (Cobain) being gone and the counterpart of that whole problem."[10] This song was written three years before Cobain died, but this anachronism aside, I do believe her when she says the song is "the counterpart of that whole problem." Bjelland had similar demons as Cobain, even down to self-medicating with heroin and other substances. I think she knew exactly what he might have felt like, because she had felt it for herself.

When she sings about things being gone, it's about one's drive and motivation. Depression can become a disembodied feeling—like you are a ghost—and the effects of Bjelland's crying chorus sounds like a haunting. The lyrics themselves are repetitious and mimic the circular thinking that so often plagues the anxious and melancholic mind. It is simple and stark in its grief and melancholy, and I think it's the album's masterpiece.

The other side of this helplessness and hopelessness is grief. It's not hard to imagine this as a dirge for the universal senselessness and randomness of death, especially given how close death surrounded the band at this time. Your loved one is gone, and there's nothing to be done about it.

And it is in a sense, as it pulls into focus the really heavier aspects of Bjelland's themes—up until now, every song has been full of fight, but at "Gone" the narrator is exhausted. Why even bother with any of this? The song ripples into stillness as a chunk of glass skips and sinks across the abyss of Bjelland's black bile.

Bruise Violet

While this is *Fontanelle*'s opening song, I've saved it for last because its oculi of controversy is in need of more healing than any other aspect of this album's story. At its core, Bjelland defined its meaning as "about doppelgängers. People trying to be like you . . . like your ghost chasing you, and you have to kill it."[11] The specter in question is named Violet, and it's been assumed this character was another famous woman musician whose betrayals of friendship are addressed in this song. Perhaps it is inspired by some of that, but true art is never only about one thing and "Bruise Violet" deserves a higher vibration in its discussion.

Violet is often a vibrant and nostalgic color that evokes the soft palettes of girlhood as well as the vintage fashions Bjelland enjoyed. As Bjelland explained, "*Violet* is just a word that a lot of girls like. It's like a ghosty spirit lady."[12] The title of "Bruise Violet" always read to me like a childhood camp story like "Bloody Mary." And I believe that story is visually alluded to within the single's video where Bjelland stands before a mirror, applying lipstick, only for her doppelgänger to flash and leave Bjelland with smudges that look like her lips have been bloodied.

Indeed, the name of "Bruise Violet" conjures an unsettling synesthesia that goes against the color's usual naïf connotations. "Bruise" is a very particular adjective of this hue—and it evokes abuse, trauma, and fury. If this is someone's name, it is obviously a moniker of a dark and sinister being.

But what if there isn't a Violet? If you pause to consider there isn't a specific person Bjelland is addressing, and that the object of rage and insult is aimed at no one but herself, the song becomes a very complicated poem of similar motifs found within the best ghost stories where narrators discover that what has been haunting aren't external manifestations, but their own inner demons. This is especially true in doppelgänger tales.

Doppelgängers are our supernatural twins, but who are never depicted as equals. One always presents something the other lacks, usually a better self, and therefore tries to dominate the weaker figure in order to exist. The only way to be rid of these malevolent doubles is to either beat them or join them. In Edgar Allan Poe's "William Wilson," the doppelgänger has to be killed so the protagonist can get on with his life, while the confined narrator in Charlotte Perkins Gilman's "The Yellow Wallpaper" sets herself free when she assumes the creeping woman's identity.

As a narrative motif, Bjelland's use of doppelgängers embodies the personification of former selves—those aspects that, no matter how badly you'd rather forget, still follow you around. For Bjelland, Violet embodies the psychic garbage in her head that she has to carry around with her every day. Within the video, her strangling her doppelgänger on the staircase is her reasserting control over herself.

"Bruise Violet" is a great choice for a lead single as it dynamically introduces *Fontanelle's* overall themes. In fact, this very idea of psychic and emotional healing is the sutures fusing all of *Fontanelle's* various themes together. All of the other songs discussed embody some various form of this existential confusion and confrontation, and are all reinforced visually by both the album's cover and its two accompanying videos. With Sherman's cover of an abandoned, naked, female doll, discarded on a chair and who affronts viewers with her anatomy, the overall concept is a foreboding yet inviting appeal to enter a haunted mind where girlhood ghosts seek healing from the unresolved traumas and tragedies of the women they grow up to be.

Plate 5
Painkillers

The Babes' story doesn't end with *Fontanelle*, but the years surrounding its making and release does encompass the apogee of their commercial career. As far as the women were concerned, it was a success, but that's because they were only ever in competition with themselves. They knew they weren't a mainstream band, and took little interest in mainstream concerns: "So for me," Herman reflected. "Success was: 'Did you make amazing records and put on great live shows? And can you make a living off touring?' Then you are successful."[1]

Even from a more mainstream perspective, she still considers it successful:

> Babes were signed long before the Nirvana feeding frenzy, so it was kind of a different situation, and there was a different expectation, but I think it did really well for a major-label debut. . . . Between Bill Bentley, the publicist . . . and Tim Carr . . . I give them so much credit. Tim just would not let up, he was going to make sure that record did not get lost in the fucking shuffle.

To Carr's credit, none of the band members seemed to know that it almost did. While he knew that the Babes wouldn't be everyone's cup of tea, the overnight, random success of Nirvana's *Nevermind*, and L7's *Bricks Are Heavy* hitting near Gold gave him confidence *Fontanelle* had the potential to sell at least 200,000 copies within the year. Everyone at Warner Brothers seemed to believe in Babes in Toyland's potential, but they were still cautious about going all in. Although Carr wanted 50,000 units made upon release, only 25,000 were printed, and to Carr's frustration, they were slow moving. Most of *Fontanelle*'s US momentum was revving up on the college radio circuit, where upon release "Bruise Violet" debuted as the #41 single out of the College Music Journal Top 150 singles for that week. It also debuted as #37 Top Cuts for College Music Journal, and within national categories, *Fontanelle* came in at #9 for Most Added Album Network Expand-O and #7 Most Added Hard Alternative (radio).[2]

But while college radio loved playing the Babes, the mainstream corporate stations did not. Even with the help of a Hit Man, these radio stations considered *Fontanelle* unlistenable to their audiences. Carr had anticipated this, and so according to Karlen, made his main promotional strategy hinge on generating "buzz" through the "Bruise Violet" video, which could only be done if it successfully aired on MTV. The buzz unfortunately revolved around a trumped up rivalry begun in a *Vanity Fair* interview between Courtney Love and Kat Bjelland. Carr sent the tape to several taste makers implying the choked-out doppelgänger was Love. This only resulted in damaging the band more than selling copies, and is an instance where I believe Carr did the band a disservice. The press pounced upon the rumor and soon it would be the only thing they wanted to discuss when it came to the band. As Herman recalled:

> It damaged Kat, the press probably gave us some notoriety in terms of name recognition, but it also cheapened us. I would go back to Chicago with all my friends and the indie rock scene and they would call us Riot Grrl. It was like . . . we used to be equals with these people and now we're a joke. Oh, you're just like Courtney.[3]

Despite this sensationalism, the video still struggled for air time. MTV rejected the video's first cut. Another version was submitted, along with Carr calling in a lot of favors and sending out a lot of swag, including four signed Cindy Sherman *Fontanelle* prints sent to the MTV execs who could make things happen.[4] "Bruise Violet" eventually aired on 120 minutes in October, and then it dropped like a dead duck off the rotation. The main avenue of promotion the band had hoped to traverse closed its roads.[5]

By October, the album had only sold 25,694 copies[6] even though *Fontanelle* was receiving rave reviews and interviews in all of the major US magazines, and *Melody Maker* and *New Musical Express* covers in Europe.[7] *Entertainment Weekly* gave it an A-,[8] while the *L.A. Times* gave it 3.5 out of 4, calling it: "the rawest performance ever released by a major label, and also one of the most necessary."[9] All of this built on top of a year's worth of glowing and positive press from *The New Yorker*, *The New York Times*, and other major publications.

Interestingly enough, *Fontanelle* was selling better abroad. Warner Brothers wasn't able to buy the Babes out of their

Southern Records contracts (which was tied with Twin/Tone) until *Nemesisters*. *Fontanelle*, then, was distributed by Southern Records, and charted #24 in the Indie UK charts.[10] The Babes began their promotional tour in England, and did amazingly well headlining sold-out shows and recording another Peel Session.

Just when buzz in the states seemed to be quieting down, the Babes were booked for the 1993 circuit of Lollapalooza. They were the first female act to be hired by the festival, a fact that was the focus of a huge publicity blitz for the band and the festival, but were then kicked off the tour half way through to make room for Tool.

While they only played the festival for a month, they optimized the opportunity beautifully. Before going on tour, the band swept into the studio to knock out a follow-up EP, *Painkillers*. It featured five songs, a re-recording of "He's My Thing," some outtakes from *Fontanelle* like "Angel Hair," and other new material like "Ishtegeit" produced by Jack Endino. On the B-side was featured *Fontanellete*, which was the epic CBGB showcase of the album done at CBGBs in April 1992. This showcase pointed new listeners, like me, back to the seminal album and this helped keep *Fontanelle*, and the Babes, from disappearing off the record store shelves entirely.

Coinciding with this, and sadly probably most significant, "Bruise Violet" was resuscitated for viewing during the twenty-fifth episode of the second season of *MTV's Beavis and Butthead* titled "Babes-R-Us."[11] Alongside White Zombie, *Beavis and Butthead* are also responsible for resurrecting interest in Babes in Toyland and *Fontanelle*. The two pubescent heroes loved the video, declaring in one glib sentence what I've spent 33,300 words trying to explain: "Woah. These chicks rock!" Herman recalls its impact feeling instantaneous: "I think I knew we were successful when my brother called me and said 'I saw you on *Beavis and Butthead*.' And that's when I knew."[12]

While the two dudes watch the video, pyro-minded Beavis misinterprets the chorus, and begins to sing "Fire!" gleefully over Bjelland's "Liar." It was this bit that would eventually lead to the video being pulled off the episode and replaced by the Butthole Surfers' "Dust Devil." A young Ohioan boy, supposedly under the cartoon's influence, set his bed on fire in October 1993, incinerating his family's home, which trapped and killed his sister. Everything that mentioned "fire" had to be purged from the previous seasons.[13]

"Babes-R-Us" appeared June 23, 1993, and as soon as it aired, Reprise cut a promo CD of the audio and circulated it to radio stations in a renewed effort to get airplay.[14] It worked: "Babes in Toyland's little-noticed 1992 LP *Fontanelle* started selling about 1,000 copies a week after the clip for 'Bruise Violet' hit *Beavis and Butt-Head*."[15] Babes in Toyland would continue to find new fans through this show. Even though "Bruise Violet" was pulled, the boys would sit down and approve of "Ripe" from *To Mother*, keeping them in rotation before the cartoon's audience, even today.

The *Beavis and Butt-head* boost eventually led to 200,000 copies of *Fontanelle* being sold both in the United States and abroad by 1994.[16] While *Fontanelle* never went Gold, it did eventually meet Tim Carr's and Warner Brothers expectations of the 200,000 units sold—having sold over 250,000 units within the United States as of 2014.[17]

Despite the band's second wind, things were beginning to get untenable for the Babes during 1993. They were going broke doing Lollapalooza thanks to label pressure to rent a huge tour bus, and the band members were beginning to feel the strain of not just constant travel but aspects of their lives they'd put on pause to get *Fontanelle* through the home stretch. Not only was Bjelland trying to establish a life with her husband in Seattle, but Barbero hadn't properly mourned the sudden loss of her father during the record-release for *Fontanelle*. Coming to terms with the Babes being their official job, Bjelland and Herman moved away from Minneapolis to try and start lives away from the band. Now they only practiced when they convened in the studio or on tour, and this only further alienated the members from each other.

While they would remain active for the next twenty years, they would never regain the momentum they had leading up to and during *Fontanelle*. Their next and last full album for Reprise would be *Nemesisters* in May 1995. After this, there was a lot of intermittent touring, with a revolving door of bassists and year-long hiatuses. After a huge 2015 reunion tour, the band officially broke up in 2017.[18]

We're All Babes in the Universe

The number of units sold is meaningless compared to the cultural impact *Fontanelle* and Babes in Toyland have had on people over the past thirty years. And to the band members, this is their ultimate measure of success and legacy. In 2021,

I asked members of Babes in Toyland how they'd like for the band to be remembered:

> **Barbero**: If we changed one person's life for the better, or . . . if we helped one person's life for the better, then I guess I'm pretty happy about that.
>
> **Leon**: I hope we continue to inspire the next generation of musicians by what we achieved, by the art we created together, those beautiful, intense, raw, powerful songs that came straight from hearts.
>
> **Herman**: I remember Babes as a band of friends who made authentic music that meant something to them and it meant something to the people that it connected with. And the band's legacy is the strength of its songs and its resonance with people. Kat was an excellent lyricist, . . . it moved people, it changed people, it gave people hope, and it gave them a voice. . . . So I think she really helped a lot of people. I think the band was a really good thing.

The Babes were a really good thing, and have continued to inspire many people for over thirty years. What is most touching about the Babes' fandom is the presence of torch passing. The original fans of Babes in Toyland are now old enough to be mothers, if not grandmothers, and it seems that they are passing the Babes' ethos down to their daughters through encouragement and promotion of their own all-girl bands. In fact, in some places little girls are born into this world guided through the birth canal by Kat Bjelland's howls:

"My daughter was born to the song 'Bruise Violet' back in 1998," writes long-time fan Carris Smith.

> When I spotted the CD player in the hospital, I was like cool I'm bringing *Fontanelle* and my daughter will be born to that! . . . My daughter Haillie (whom I wanted to name Violet but it got shot down) grew up with Babes in Toyland, and when she was little called it "crazy music." Now she is just as huge a fan. . . . I have done my best to pass down the legacy of Babes in Toyland and I will continue to cherish the music.[19]

When the Babes stopped recording in 1996, their influence was not silenced, but merely laid dormant in record stores and re-runs of *Beavis and Butthead, 1991: The Year Punk Broke*, and other venues, just waiting for the right person to find them. Everyday someone is discovering Babes in Toyland for themselves, and it is always described as an awakening. Smith discovered Babes in Toyland in 1993 via the "Bruise Violet" video that was airing on Much Music at a friend's house. She was immediately drawn to the imagery and the music, and was gifted *Fontanelle* for her sweet sixteen.

> It was like it was written especially for me. . . . Every time I listened to their music I heard something new, I could twist the lyrics to whatever I was feeling that day. It saved me numerous times. I was a very depressed/suicidal teenager, and listening to music was my only outlet. It was reassuring that someone else out there seemed to understand me.

Truth is, whether its 1992 or 2022, being a thirteen-year-old girl is a universally painful experience. Boys are forever getting their angst outlets through music, but up until Babes in Toyland, and the bands that followed afterwards in the early 1990s, music did not offer that same sort of catharsis for women. Bjelland's songs revealed taboo topics that teenage girls and young women could identify with much like Plath's poetry did for Bjelland's generation. For Brazilian writer, critic, and zinester Larissa Oliveira, who discovered Babes in Toyland in 2011 at the age of sixteen, she found *Fontanelle* a much-needed beacon to navigate her adolescence:

> It's an album that will impact a lot young girls who are dealing with lots in their lives. . . . I had so much inside of me that I couldn't let out because I was a girl in a strict catholic family from the smallest state of Brazil. You can't stay neutral after such an intense experience that is listening to Babes in Toyland.

While the experiences will vary, the emotions all stem from the same violent shadow space that Bjelland and Babes in Toyland explored in their music. You realize that you, too, can be angry, scream, and protest. That you can stand up for yourself, your friends, and lift other people up.

The greatest legacy between Babes in Toyland and their fans is their DIY ethos that inspires people to pick up an instrument and teaching yourself to play. Despite their disdain for perfectionism, the example they set included the following principles: to not be afraid to fail or make mistakes, that excellence comes from years of practice, perseverance, and experimentation, and to never compete with others, only compete with yourself. The Babes' embraced imperfections in their music, and considered them just a further form of pure expression. Their mistakes, then, were their greatness, and in a world that daily emphasizes a distorted notion of professionalism and expertise, this is the ultimate permission. It reminds us that you have to start somewhere and that regardless of gender norms and societal mores you have a right to whatever space it is you want to explore.

With these positive directives, it's no wonder Babes in Toyland has influenced not just nineties bands like Hole, Bikini Kill, and Sleater-Kinney, but many bands since. There are the neo-riot grrl bands like Skating Polly (whose bassist Clara Sayler stepped in to replace Herman in 2015 for the reunion tour), Slutever, and Minneapolis-based Bruise Violet. There's also White Lung, whose lead singer Mish Way has written several kudos crediting Babes in Toyland's influence on her music, Hag Face, Witch Fever, Deap Valley, Calico Fray, Margarita Podridas, Los Bitchos, and Skinny Girl Diet.

Arta Salehi, the guitarist and vocalist for Quinn the Brain, cites Babes in Toyland as a liberation from her own self-doubts when it came to singing, songwriting, and making music:

It felt like I was listening to art. Before Babes in Toyland, I thought songs were written a certain way. They had to follow a certain formula and the guitars had to have solos to be considered good. After Babes in Toyland, I realized there were no rules. You didn't need a solo or even a melody to sound good. It just opened up this door that I didn't realize existed, and I was able to tap into my most creative self . . . Lori's drums were a game changer. I didn't realize how much I loved toms until I heard Lori play. I now find myself always wanting more toms in every song because of her.

Dana S, from Phoenix, AZ, discovered Babes in Toyland through a used promo copy of *Fontanelle*. She describes the experience of hearing them for the first time as many others have, as an awakening force:

On an artistic level, hearing Babes 100% inspired me to pick up my dust infested guitar and actually try to write songs, or at least make some noise. I really connected with the primal (in every way) nature of their music and wanted to see if I could do that, too. On a personal level, Babes in Toyland have definitely influenced and inspired me. I began to realize that I could take and use the dark parts in me and channel them out in a way that worked for ME. I could take those things out of my head and twist and turn them into something I could send outward rather than keeping it all buried. These dark parts could actually be used for something positive.

But Babes' has inspired others to stoke these same flames within other genres. In the case of Oliveira, Jessica Hopper, and myself, it has been through writing. For others, like Brett Rothrock, it's through the visual arts. Rothrock discovered the Babes in 2007, and they have had a seminal influence on his photography ever since:

I think they represent an aggressive confidence and originality that is rare in art . . . They certainly had the talent as musicians, but they were able to twist preconceptions and expectations in a way that sounded brand new and different and they did it seamlessly. They were, in many ways, a shock to the collective system which I think left many people baffled. But by being themselves in doing what they did, I think they had a tremendous impact on many artists, bands, and people, both male and female.

Boto (W)rap Up

How do you describe an auditory tornado like *Fontanelle*? Steam roller riffs, skull hammering beats, and the Banshee-Siren maelstrom of Kat Bjelland screaming, swearing, pleading, and bleeding all over the studio? Distortion and discord parting and mingling with fragile melody and lyrics hardened by wit and irony to hide the vulnerable, gooey uncertainties in the middle?

Everything—from the soft surrealist lyrics, to their album names and song titles, to their girlhood violence—all suggested and destroyed the notion of femaleness. It was this double-edged femininity that I was first drawn to as a teen, and I'd continue to be drawn to and utilize to express my own art. It was like all the anger, confusion, frustration, and ambivalence I felt then were justified because these women not only felt it to, but were able to transform it into a magical catharsis.

It was a presentation of a space I didn't know existed, much less that I could have access to. A space that, up until that moment, I'd seen occupied by men, and here were full-grown women performing this art harder and more uniquely than their counterparts. And they did all this without apology, and simply because they believed they could.

These were examples of a future womanhood I could aspire to, and it would set examples for others as well. And while Babes in Toyland were never a feminist project, it is because of them that I became a feminist. I had no idea in 1993 how loaded of a word that was, and how loaded of a word it would continue to be, even now in 2022. What I became after hearing the Babes wasn't about theory, or waves, or movements, but about practice and attitude. It was about gaining confidence that I not only had a place in the world but I had the right to occupy it. My personal feminism was built upon the foundations of their noise that signaled to me that despite external restrictions, absolute freedom could be found through artistic action.

Babes in Toyland's art is amoral, but as such is about truth. It doesn't aim to make political commentary but personal testimony. Through these fly-on-the-wall depictions, there are no manifestos or definitive statements of what the experience of womanhood should or shouldn't be, but just what it is through the lens of their lives. This radical intimacy holds up a mirror for us to examine ourselves in ways that society would rather we all ignored. But once we've faced these truths, we can integrate these shadows into a more productive and progressive escape from the same sinkholes society tried to suck women down in 1993 and is still trying to suck us down today.

Fontanelle has remained a timeless reminder that no matter how much certain demographics may want it, women are not dolls designed to play house inside the patriarchy. What this album did for me at twelve years old still serves me at forty. I expected by now to be less angry, less annoyed, less bothered by the ignored achievements and diminishment of my and other women's choices, but, it's only become worse. More than ever, I need strength, I need rage, I need wrath to just get through the day. I need to hear and see women unleash their inner banshees, to reclaim their Sirenhood, to look into the eyes of the medusa and risk petrification for a fucking hug, because I need their screams to prevail.

Babes in Toyland were formed during a time when the word "feminism" felt unnecessary to most women, because it felt like the second wave had won. But by *Fontanelle's* release, in 1992, those strides were being cast in doubt by a systematic conservative backlash designed to make women lose faith in their own individualism outside of the home. This backlash primarily used motherhood and children as its emotional warfare, and this is when abortion clinics began being bombed, doctors were assassinated, laws chiseled away at Roe v. Wade, and overall women were gaslit into forgoing their choices be it reproductive or professional.[20] But, despite all of this, the next generation of women who made up the third wave rejected all of these societal ploys to unlock the ideas of feminism at a personal rather than intellectual core. They fought against the backlash, but it would rise again, stronger and stealthier, against the third and fourth waves. Now, in 2022, it has breached the dam.

That is why we need to hear Bjelland screech things like "You don't try to rape a Goddess." It is a reminder that women have always had and continue to have the capacity for power over themselves, that they don't have to remain in a passive state, that they don't need authorities' permission to live their lives as they wish. Through art and catharsis, they are as capable of action, protection, and self-celebration as anyone else. Babes in Toyland demonstrates the power and possibility of female rage and the needed space for this expression. It's a space that now, more than ever, women are going to need.

♪

Notes

Intro

1 Charlotte Richardson Andrews, "Cult Heroes: Babes in Toyland's Kat Bjelland—Overlooked 90s Punk Powerhouse," *The Guardian,* February 3, 2015. https://www.theguardian.com /music/2015/feb/03/cult-heroes-babes-in-toylands-kat-bjelland -overlooked-90s-punk-powerhouse. Accessed May 7, 2020.

2 Suzy Exposito, "50 Greatest Grunge Albums," *Rolling Stone,* April 1, 2019. https://www.rollingstone.com/music/music -lists/50-greatest-grunge-albums-798851/babes-in-toyland -fontanelle-1992-798848/. Accessed March 7, 2021.

3 Melanie Beasley, "Age of Closure of Fontanelles / Sutures," The Center for Academic Research and Training in Anthropogeny. http://carta.anthropogeny.org/moca/topics/age-closure -fontanelles-sutures. Accessed May 18, 2022.

4 Neal Karlen was very gracious enough to discuss these matters with me in an interview conducted on January 23, 2022.

5 The media often depicted the band's name as an obvious reference to the band members' gender. In retaliation, Bjelland

would explain that "Babes" alluded to the innocence and wonder of babies. She would explain that all gender and all people were "babes in the universe."

Plate 1

1   Author interview with Lori Barbero, conducted April 16, 2021.

2   "A Conversation with Lori Barbero of Babes in Toyland," MN Music Coalition YouTube Channel, August 3, 2018. https://youtu.be/9ycXPPjjnTI. Accessed February 11, 2021.

3   "Babes in Toyland Interview with Kat and Lori (1992)," Originally appeared on MTV 120 minutes. Kerry's Rarities YouTube Channel. https://youtu.be/C3RKxYTkC94. Accessed July 19, 2021.

4   J. Free, "An Interview/Conversation with Kat Bjelland of Babes In Toyland," Originally appeared in The New Puritan Review, January 1990. Reprinted at Sonic Archives. https://www.sonicarchives.com/taste/pgs/npr_bbtd.php. Accessed May 19, 2021.

5   Liz Evans, *Women, Sex, and Rock and Roll: In Their Own Words* (London: Pandora, 1994), 64.

6   Free, "An Interview/Conversation with Kat Bjelland of Babes In Toyland."

7   David Higginbotham, AMA within comments of "The Venarays | Kat Bjelland | Full interview & Performances," Glittersister YouTube channel, May 10, 2021. https://www.youtube.com/watch?v=8NJXuNwH9Y0. Accessed May 21, 2021.

8   Ibid.

9   John Peel and Kat Bjelland BBC Radio One Interview from August 28, 1993. "John Peel's Interview - Babes in Toyland," John Peel YouTube Channel, https://youtu.be/RWgk642A67o. Accessed May 19, 2021.

10 Alex Woodward, "Interview: Babes in Toyland's Kat Bjelland on the Band's Second Coming," *Gambit*, October 27, 2015. https://www.nola.com/gambit/music/article_eaa08db0-a1c8 -5a35-8e1e-afe812654993.html. Accessed December 1, 2021.

11 Evans, *Women, Sex, and Rock and Roll*. 64.

12 "The Venarays | Kat Bjelland | Full Interview & Performances," Glittersister YouTube Channel, May 10, 2021. https://www .youtube.com/watch?v=8NJXuNwH9Y0. Accessed May 21, 2021.

13 Erika Meyer, "Introducing Napalm Beach," https://www .seastorm.com/napalm_beach_history.html. Accessed December 1, 2021.

14 Evans, *Women, Sex, and Rock and Roll*, 65.

15 Ibid., 66.

16 "Courtney Love + The Story of Sugar Babydoll," GrrlBandGeek Youtube Channel. https://www.youtube.com/ watch?v=u-Hsx3Zizdo. Accessed May 11, 2021.

17 Andrea Swennson, "Kat Bjelland on Babes in Toyland and her Long and Winding Career," *The* Current, March 10, 2013. https://www.thecurrent.org/feature/2013/03/10/kat-bjelland -on-babes-in-toyland-and-her-long-and-winding-career. Accessed May 11, 2021.

18 Martin Donohoe, "Pagan Babies," *Bernadine*. https://web .archive.org/web/20110812085950/http://bernadine.eu.pn/ paganbabies.htm. Accessed May 11, 2021.

19 Gerry McGovern, "Wild Women Never Die," Hot Press, April 2, 2001. https://www.hotpress.com/music/wild-women-never-die-459975 Accessed January 12, 2022.

20 "A Conversation with Lori Barbero of Babes in Toyland," MN Music Coalition YouTube Channel, August 3, 2018. https://youtu.be/9ycXPPjjnTI. Accessed February 11, 2021.

21 Evans, *Women, Sex, and Rock and Roll*, 67.

22 Cecilia Johnson and Michelangelo Matos, "October 22, 1990: Sonic Youth/Cows/Babes in Toyland," The Current, October 20, 2020. https://www.thecurrent.org/episode/2020/10/20/oct-22-1990-sonic-youth-cows-babes-in-toyland. Accessed May 10, 2021.

23 Author interview with Michelle Leon, conducted May 14, 2021.

24 Michelle Leon, *I Live Inside: Memoirs of a Babe in Toyland* (St. Paul: Minnesota Historical Society Press, 2016), 20.

25 Ibid.

26 "A Conversation with Lori Barbero of Babes in Toyland," MN Music Coalition YouTube Channel, August 3, 2018. https://youtu.be/9ycXPPjjnTI. Accessed February 11, 2021.

27 Lizzie Ehrenhalt, "From a Minneapolis Art Gallery's Basement to the Heights of the Alternative Rock Scene: Babes in Toyland," *MinnPost*, February 20, 2017. https://www.minnpost.com/mnopedia/2017/02/minneapolis-art-gallery-s-basement-heights-alternative-rock-scene-babes-toyland/. Accessed May 18, 2021.

28 Dina Gachman, "The Riot Grrrl, The Activist, The Punk Singer: Interview with Kathleen Hanna," *The Hairpin*, November 26, 2013. https://www.thehairpin.com/2013/11/the-riot-grrrl-the-activist-the-punk-singer-interview-with-kathleen-hanna/. Accessed December 7, 2021.

29   Michelle, *I Live Inside,* 23.

30   Author interview with Lori Barbero, conducted April 16, 2021.

31   "Babes in Toyland interview Request Video," Callye's Live and Rare Music Vids YouTube Channel. https://youtu.be/D2su-_SmRBQ. Accessed May 19, 2021.

32   "A Conversation with Lori Barbero of Babes in Toyland," MN Music Coalition YouTube Channel, August 3, 2018. https://youtu.be/9ycXPPjjnTI. Accessed February 11, 2021.

33   Michelle, *I Live Inside,* 22.

34   "Lori Barbero of Babes in Toyland, the Complete Interview from Color Me Obsessed," Gorman Bechard YouTube Channel. https://youtu.be/lEOX4Aw4H0o. Accessed December 21, 2021.

35   Author interview with Michelle Leon, conducted May 14, 2021.

36   Free, "An Interview/Conversation with Kat Bjelland of Babes in Toyland."

37   Richard Cromelin, "Year of the Kat: Kat Bjelland's Penchant for Purging her Emotions Brings Babes in Toyland to the Brink of Alternative Rock Stardom," *L.A. Times*, November 15, 1992. https://www.latimes.com/archives/la-xpm-1992-11-15-ca-623-story.html. Accessed August 14, 2021.

38   "Babes in Toyland - Kat Bjelland About Possession // Not bad for a Girl Documentary," Breno Valli YouTube Channel. https://www.youtube.com/watch?v=nHsAipVtqKU. Accessed May 19, 2021.

Plate 2

1   Megan Matuzak, "Q & A with Babes in Toyland's Kat Bjelland," *Phawker*, October 21, 2015. http://www.phawker

.com/2015/10/21/qa-with-babes-in-toylands-kat-bjelland/. Accessed May 19, 2021.

2 Michelle Leon, *I Live Inside: Memoirs of a Babe in Toyland* (St. Paul: Minnesota Historical Society Press, 2016), 22.

3 Ibid., 30.

4 "Babes In Toyland - Cabooze Bar, Minneapolis 1988," Glaucco Emmanual YouTube Channel. https://youtu.be/KGPOC26rxYQ. Accessed December 6, 2021.

5 "Babes in Toyland Live October 29th 1988, Uptown Bar, Minneapolis," Wership YouTube channel. https://youtu.be/dmXLQgUNS6Y. Accessed December 6, 2021.

6 Author interview with Lori Barbero, conducted April 16, 2021.

7 Neal Karlen, *Babes in Toyland: The Making and Selling of a Rock and Roll Band* (New York: Times Books, 1994), 38–9.

8 "Babes in Toyland Concert Setlists & Tour Dates," *Setlist.fm.* https://www.setlist.fm/setlists/babes-in-toyland-13d68901.html?page=52. Accessed April 2, 2022.

9 Leon, *I Live Inside,* 52.

10 Author interview with Lori Barbero, conducted April 16, 2021.

11 Author interview with Lori Barbero, conducted April 16, 2021.

12 Cecilia Johnson and Michelangelo Matos, "October 22, 1990: Sonic Youth/Cows/Babes in Toyland," The Current, October 20, 2020. https://www.thecurrent.org/episode/2020/10/20/oct-22-1990-sonic-youth-cows-babes-in-toyland. Accessed May 10, 2021.

13 J. Free, "An Interview/Conversation with Kat Bjelland of Babes in Toyland," Originally appeared in The New Puritan

Review, January 1990. Reprinted at Sonic Archives. https://www.sonicarchives.com/taste/pgs/npr_bbtd.php. Accessed May 19, 2021.

14 Ibid.

15 Author interview with Brian Paulson, conducted February 16, 2022.

16 Leon, *I Live Inside*, 38.

17 Matuzak, "Q & A with Babes in Toyland's Kat Bjelland."

18 Leon, *I Live Inside*, 166.

19 Author interview with Brian Paulson, conducted February 16, 2022.

20 Various authors, "In Their Voices: Babes in Toyland's Lasting Impression on Women in Twin Cities Music," *The Star Tribune*, June 30, 2015. https://www.startribune.com/in-their-voices-babes-in-toyland-s-lasting-impression-on-women-in-twin-cities-music/308196071/. Accessed April 9, 2022.

21 Leon, *I Live Inside*, 89–90.

22 Author interview with Jack Endino, conducted throughout August 2021.

23 Ibid.

24 Leon, *I Live Inside*, 90.

25 Author interview with Lee Ranaldo, conducted January 29, 2022.

26 EW Staff, "Notable Music for the Week of April 27, 1990," *Entertainment Weekly*, April 27, 1990. https://ew.com/article/1990/04/27/notable-music-week-april-27-1990-0/. Accessed May 21, 2021.

27 Karlen, *Babes in Toyland*, 165.

28 "Babes in Toyland-To Mother (vinyl)," SouthernRecords
    .com, September 13, 2016. https://web.archive.org/web
    /20160913164425/http://shop.southern.com/babes-in-toyland
    -to-mother-vinyl/. Accessed May 19, 2022.

29 Thurston Moore, "Ex-Sonic Youth Man Thurston Moore on
    Why Babes in Toyland are Still One of Punks Most Incendiary
    Forces," *NME.com*, May 28, 2015. https://www.nme.com/blogs
    /nme-blogs/ex-sonic-youth-man-thurston-moore-on-why
    -babes-in-toyland-are-still-one-of-punks-most-incendiary-for
    -17151. Accessed May 19, 2021.

30 Liz Evans, *Women, Sex, and Rock and Roll: In Their Own
    Words* (London: Pandora, 1994), 68.

31 Moore, "Ex-Sonic Youth Man Thurston Moore on Why Babes
    in Toyland are Still One of Punks Most Incendiary Forces."

32 Author interview with Michelle Leon, conducted May 14,
    2021.

Anterior Fontanelle

1 Kat Bjelland, "Babes in Toyland," dustcakegrrl138. YouTube
   Channel. https://youtu.be/w14_NF0SGPs. Sept 2 2012.
   Accessed August 13, 2021.

2 Author interview with Lori Barbero, conducted April 16,
   2021.

3 *Not Bad for a Girl*. Directed by Lisa Rose Apramian. Spitshine
   Productions. 1995.

4 Lori Barbero, "Babes in Toyland," dustcakegrrl138. YouTube
   Channel, September 2 2012. https://youtu.be/w14_NF0SGPs.
   Accessed August 13, 2021.

5   Hannah was not clear when the show was, and the Babes were touring the Pacific Northwest throughout April 1990. Bikini Kill was formed in 1990, and so I am assuming that this house show had to have occurred around this time.

6   "Kathleen Hannah: Love, Lyrics & Babes in Toyland," *Conversations with Bianca,* February 12, 2012. https://conversationswithbianca.com/2012/02/12/kathleen-hanna/. Accessed February 18, 2022.

7   Kathleen Hannah, Liner notes essay. *The Best of Babes in Toyland and Kat Bjelland.* Southern Records (Warner Brothers Music UK Ltd., 2004. CD).

8   "Kathleen Hannah: Love, Lyrics & Babes in Toyland." *Conversations with Bianca,* February 12, 2012. https://conversationswithbianca.com/2012/02/12/kathleen-hanna/. Accessed February 18, 2022.

9   Mish Way, "Mis Way (White Lung) Talks About Screaming It Out," *Talkhouse,* May 11, 2013. https://www.talkhouse.com/mish-way-white-lung-talks-about-screaming-it-out/. Accessed May 19, 2021.

10 Maureen Herman, "Babes in Toyland," dustcakegrrl138. YouTube Channel, September 2 2012. https://youtu.be/w14_NF0SGPs. Accessed August 13, 2021.

11 Jessica Hopper, *The First Collection of Criticism by a Living Female Rock Critic: Revised and Expanded* (New York: Farrar, Straus and Giroux, 2021). Kindle edition, section 4833–8.

    Hopper saw the band when she was 15 in 1990, and disappointed in the media's inability to cover them as more than an all-girl novelty, she was inspired to start her own zine, *Hit It or Quit It.* This became a flagship zine for riot grrrl culture, and a watershed moment for criticism of women in music.

12 *Not Bad for a Girl*. Directed by Lisa Rose Apramian. Spitshine Productions. 1995.

13 Michelle Leon, *I Live Inside: Memoirs of a Babe in Toyland* (St. Paul: Minnesota Historical Society Press, 2016), 90.

14 Taken by Dan Corrigan.

15 *Not Bad for a Girl*. Directed by Lisa Rose Apramian. Spitshine Productions. 1995.

16 Leon, *I Live Inside*, 114.

17 Liz Evans, *Women, Sex, and Rock and Roll: In Their Own Words* (London: Pandora, 1994), 62.

18 Ibid.

19 Daniel Fidler, "Babes 'R Us," *Spin,* September 1992, 30.

20 Thurston Moore, "Ex-Sonic Youth Man Thurston Moore on Why Babes in Toyland Are Still One of Punk's Most Incendiary Force," *NME.com,* May 28, 2015. https://www.nme .com/blogs/nme-blogs/ex-sonic-youth-man-thurston-moore -on-why-babes-in-toyland-are-still-one-of-punks-most -incendiary-for-17151. Accessed May 19, 2021.

Plate 3

1 Neal Karlen, *Babes in Toyland: The Making and Selling of a Rock and Roll Band* (New York: Times Books, 1994), 42–3, 48–9 and 51–2.

2 Hillary Hughes, "How the Go-Go's Perfected Punk," NPR, August 5, 2020. https://www.npr.org/2020/08/05/898998568

/how-the-go-gos-perfected-pop-punk. Accessed March 12, 2022.

3 Kelly McCartney, *Medium*. "*The Origin of the Bangles*," June 5, 2015. https://medium.com/cuepoint/ladies-and-gentlemen -the-bangles-7450982ae099. Accessed March 12, 2022.

4 Alex Woodward, "Interview: Babes in Toyland's Kat Bjelland on the Band's Second Coming," *Gambit*, October 27, 2015. https://www.nola.com/gambit/music/article_eaa08db0-a1c8 -5a35-8e1e-afe812654993.html. Accessed December 1, 2021.

5 Shawn Conner, "Still Rocking: Babes in Toyland Vocalist Kat Bjelland Talks About Touring After 20 Years," *The Vancouver Sun*, September 1, 2015. https://vancouversun.com /entertainment/music/still-rocking-babes-in-toyland-vocalist -kat-bjelland-talks-about-touring-after-20-years. Accessed August 14, 2021.

6 Author interview with Lori Barbero, conducted April 16, 2021.

7 Paul Schmelzer. "'Completely Punk Rock': Cindy Sherman's (Nearly) Forgotten History with Babes in Toyland," The Walker Art Center, February 7, 2013. https://walkerart.org /magazine/cindy-sherman-babes-in-toyland-punk-rock. Accessed January 20, 2022.

8 Author interview with Lori Barbero, conducted April 16, 2021.

9 Rasmus Holmen, "The Money Will Roll Right In," The Internet Nirvana Fan Club. https://www.nirvanaclub.com /get.php?section=info/general&file=money.htm. Accessed January 21, 2022.

10 Alec Foege, *Confusion Is Next: The Sonic Youth Story* (New York: St. Martin's Press, 1994), 199–202.

11 Karlen, *Babes in Toyland,* 58–9, 65 and 118.

12 Author interview with Lori Barbero, conducted April 16, 2021.

13 "Babes in Toyland. Babes in Toyland-Bloomington (1991, DHV 2012)," *Late Night Snack TV Show, 21 May 1991.* István Császár YouTube Channel, December 14, 2014. https://youtu.be/aOk-2Z80Zds. Accessed May 21, 2021.

14 Michelle Leon, *I Live Inside: Memoirs of a Babe in Toyland* (St. Paul: Minnesota Historical Society Press, 2016), 168–9.

15 "Babes In Toyland—1992 EP (Bruise Violet, Magick Flute, Gone)," Kerry's Rarities YouTube Channel, August 22, 2021. https://youtu.be/_EfDibPi3KE. Accessed January 21, 2022.

16 Author interview with Lee Ranaldo, conducted January 29, 2022.

17 Ibid.

18 Karlen, *Babes in Toyland*, 63 and Leon, *I Live Inside*, 121.

19 Ibid., 152.

20 Karlen, *Babes in Toyland,* 68.

21 Ibid., 77.

22 Leon, *I Live Inside*, 161.

23 Author interview with Michelle Leon, conducted May 14, 2021.

24 Brian Escamilla, *Contemporary Musician* (Detroit: Gale Research, Inc., 1996), 7.

25 Mark Yarm, "Everybody Loves Our Outakes, Horrifying Kitchen Accident Edition: Babes in Toyland's Maureen Herman on Starting Bass," *Everybody Loves Our Town,* March 7, 2012. https://grungebook.tumblr.com/post/18904097082/babes-in-toyland-maureen-herman-on-starting-bass. Accessed February 10, 2022.

26   Author interview with Maureen Herman, conducted January 23, 2022.

27   Matthew Larman-Smith, "Interview with Maureen Herman, July 1993," *Smithlahrman.blogspot.com,* September 23, 2011. http://smithlahrman.blogspot.com/2011/09/interview-with -maureen-herman-july-1993.html. Accessed May 16, 2020.

28   Author interview with Maureen Herman, conducted January 23, 2022.

29   Ibid.

30   Ibid.

31   Ibid.

Plate 4

1   Neal Karlen, *Babes in Toyland: The Making and Selling of a Rock and Roll Band* (New York: Times Books, 1994), 112–13.

2   Unless cited otherwise, all quotes in this and the previous chapter are from interviews with the author from 2021 to 2022.

3   Karlen, *Babes in Toyland,* 140–1.

4   Ibid.

5   Ibid., 141.

6   Ibid.

Posterior Fontanelle

1   Liz Evans, *Women, Sex, and Rock and Roll: In Their Own Words* (London: Pandora, 1994), 61.This wonderful book was

one of the few resources I've found where Bjelland opens up about her songwriting intent and process.

2 Ibid., 71.

3 Ibid., 70.

4 Sylvia Plath, "Medusa," In *Sylvia Plath: The Collected Poems,* ed. Ted Hughes (New York: Harper Collins, 2018), 225.

5 Neal Karlen, *Babes in Toyland: The Making and Selling of a Rock and Roll Band* (New York: Times Books, 1994), 161–2.

6 Evans, *Women, Sex, and Rock and Roll,* 68.

7 Richard Nanian, "Humours," George Mason University. http://mason.gmu.edu/~rnanian/humours.html. Accessed June 16, 2022.

8 "A History of the Liver, Gall Bladder, and Spleen," Stanford University. https://web.stanford.edu/class/history13/earlysciencelab/body/liverpages/livergallbladderspleen.html. Accessed June 16, 2022.

9 C. E. Woodman, "Easter and the Ecclesiastical Calendar," *Journal of the Royal Astronomical Society of Canada* 17 (May 1923): 41.

10 Megan Matuzak, "Q & A with Babes in Toyland's Kat Bjelland," Phawker, October 21, 2015. http://www.phawker.com/2015/10/21/qa-with-babes-in-toylands-kat-bjelland/. Accessed May 19, 2021.

11 Gillian G. Gaar, *She's a Rebel: The History of Women in Rock & Roll,* 2nd ed. (New York: Seal Press, 2002), 391.

12 Chris Mundy, "Q&A with Kat Bjelland of Babes in Toyland," *Rolling Stone,* May 18, 1995. https://www.rollingstone.com/music/music-news/qa-kat-bjelland-of-babes-in-toyland-65900/. Accessed May 17, 2021.

Plate 5

1   Author interview with Maureen Herman, conducted January 23, 2022.

2   Neal Karlen, *Babes in Toyland: The Making and Selling of a Rock and Roll Band* (New York: Times Books, 1994), 214–15, 221–22 and 228.

3   Author interview with Maureen Herman, conducted January 23, 2022.

4   I've always felt like people never knew what they had with Babes in Toyland. Case in point, one of these signed prints went up for auction at Christies' sixteen years later. While estimated to be worth $3–4,000, it was sold for a measly $750.

5   Karlen, *Babes in Toyland,* 224–7.

6   Ibid., 229.

7   Ibid., 212–3.

8   Arion Berger, "Fontanelle," *Entertainment Weekly,* August 28, 1992. https://ew.com/article/1992/08/28/fontanelle/. Accessed June 18, 2022.

9   Jonathan Gold, "Anger from the Anti-Bangles," *Los Angeles Times,* August 30, 1992. https://www.latimes.com/archives/la-xpm-1992-08-30-ca-8261-story.html. Accessed June 18, 2022.

10 "Babes in Toyland," The Official Charts Company. https://www.officialcharts.com/artist/4636/babes-in-toyland/. Accessed June 18, 2022.

11 "Babes R' Us," *Beavis and Butt-Head Wiki.* https://beavisandbutthead.fandom.com/wiki/Babes_%27R%27_Us. Accessed June 18, 2022.

12   Author interview with Maureen Herman, conducted January 23, 2022.

13   Brian Boone, "The Untold Truth of Beavis and Butt-head," Looper.com, April 1, 2022. https://www.looper.com/173544/the-untold-truth-of-beavis-and-butt-head/. Accessed May 29, 2022.

14   "Beavis and Butt-head in Toyland: Bruise Violet," Promotional CD 1993. DOABloodrock YouTube Channel, February 26, 2012. https://youtu.be/5QTZUixnQAU. Accessed May 29, 2022.

15   Boone, "The Untold Truth of Beavis and Butt-head."

16   Karlen, *Babes in Toyland*, 287.

17   Andrew Earles, *Gimme Indie Rock* (New York: Voyageur Press, 2014), 24.

18   Lori Barbero, *Conan Neutral's Protonic Reversal Podcast*. Episode 166. May 24, 2020. Accessed December 14, 2020.

19   All fan quotes are from interviews with the author conducted via email in 2022.

20   Susan Faludi, *Backlash: The Undeclared War Against American Women* (New York: Broadway Books, 2020).

Selected Bibliography

Clark, Heather. *Red Comet: The Short Life and Blazing Art of Sylvia Plath*. New York: Vintage, 2021.

Evans, Liz. *Women, Sex, and Rock and Roll: In Their Own Words*. London: Pandora, 1994.

Faludi, Susan. *Backlash: The Undeclared War Against American Women*. New York: Broadway Books, 2020.

Gaar, Gillian G. *She's a Rebel: The History of Women in Rock & Roll*, 2nd ed. New York: Seal Press, 2002.

Goldman, Vivien. *Revenge of the She Punks: A Feminist Music History from Poly Styrene to Pussy Riot*. Chicago: University of Chicago Press, 2019.

Hopper, Jessica. *The First Collection of Criticism by a Living Female Rock Critic: Revised and Expanded*. New York: Farrar, Straus and Giroux, 2021.

Karlen, Neal. *Babes in Toyland: The Making and Selling of a Rock and Roll Band*. New York: Times Books, 1994.

Leon, Michelle. *I Live Inside: Memoirs of a Babe in Toyland*. St. Paul: Minnesota Historical Society Press, 2016.

Meltzer, Marisa. *Girl Power: The Nineties Revolution in Music*. New York: Farrar, Straus and Giroux, 2010.

SELECTED BIBLIOGRAPHY

O'Brien, Lucy. *She Bop: The Definitive History of Women in Popular Music, Revised and Updated 25th edition*. London: Jawbone Press, 2020.

Plath, Sylvia. *Sylvia Plath: The Collected Poems*. Edited by Ted Hughes. New York: Harper Collins, 2018.

Yarm, Mark. *Everybody Loves Out Town: An Oral History of Grunge*. New York: Crown, 2012.

Acknowledgments

I am eternally grateful to Lori Barbero, Jack Endino, Maureen Herman, Michelle Leon, Neal Karlen, Brian Paulson, and Lee Ranaldo for making time to share their memories, experiences, and perspectives with me during the pandemic. There is no way I could have written this book without those conversations. While I was unable to establish contact with Kat Bjelland to discuss this book, her flame burned vehemently while I wrote and I am forever grateful for the pleasure and power her music has given me. I also would like to thank my editors Leah Babb-Rosenfeld for her patience and support; Rachel Moore for her guidance; and to Dr. Samantha Bennett who understood my vision and passion for the Babes, and helped me further define and refine it into its final form. I am very grateful for the keen eyes and polish of Elizabeth Kellingley and Vishnu Prasad, and for the entire Bloomsbury Academic teams (both US and UK) who helped me usher this book along into the world.

Huge shout-out to the fans of Babes in Toyland rock my world!!!! Facebook group, where some of its members graciously granted me interviews and whose excitement kept me going on this long project. Dana S, Brett Rothrock,

Carris Smith, Larissa Oliveira, and Arta Salehi—thank you for sharing your love of the Babes with me.

I was very fortunate to have a solid support system behind me as I wrote this: my family: Joshua Johnson, Baby Kat Chambers-Johnson, and Kent Chambers (who took me to see the Babes in 1994); and my friends Mike Allen, Carrie Ann Baade, Jesse Bullington, Nicole Caputo, Peter D'Ettore, Stacy and Lesli Froeschner, Jason Heller, Jen and Tim Schomburg Kanke, Nick Mamatas, Daniel Pearce and Saba Shariat-Pearce, Ben Pilat, Thomas Poucher, Angie Sigg, Molly Tanzer, and Marshall Wiseheart. Thank you all for hanging in there with me.

Author Bio

Selena Chambers is the author of *Calls for Submission* (Pelekinesis) and *Wandering Spirits: Traveling Mary Shelley's Frankenstein* (TallHat Press). Her fiction and nonfiction have been nominated for the Pushcart, Colorado Book Award, Best of the Net, as well as the Hugo Award and World Fantasy award (twice). Her work has also been translated in France, Spain, Brazil, and Turkey, and has published in the UK and Australia. She lives with her partner and fur-daughter in the Florida Panhandle.

Also Available in the Series